DR. ODWA GULWA

STOP WORKING
GET WEALTHY

Is Your JOB Stopping You
from Becoming Wealthy?

Copyright © 2018 by Dr. Odwa Gulwa

STOP WORKING GET WEALTHY

All rights reserved. No part of this publication may be reproduced, distributed, or transmitted in any form or by any means, including photocopying, recording, or other electronic or mechanical methods, without the prior written permission of the publisher, except in the case of brief quotations embodied in critical reviews and certain other noncommercial uses permitted by copyright law. For permission requests, write to the publisher, addressed "Attention: Permissions Coordinator," at info@beyondpublishing.net

Quantity sales special discounts are available on quantity purchases by corporations, associations, and others. For details, contact the publisher at the address above.

Cover and text design © 2018 by Grzegorz Japoł (grzegorz.japol@gmail.com)

Orders by U.S. trade bookstores and wholesalers.
Email info@BeyondPublishing.net

The Beyond Publishing Speakers Bureau can bring authors to your live event. For more information or to book an event contact the Beyond Publishing Speakers Bureau speak@BeyondPublishing.net

The Author can be reached directly BeyondPublishing.net/AuthorDrOdwaGulwa

Manufactured and printed in the United States of America distributed globally by BeyondPublishing.net

New York | Los Angeles | London | Sydney

ISBN: 978-0-720-81280-0

To my fiancé and children:
Thank you for putting up with
me and adding immensely to my heart
wealth.

To everyone who kept asking where the book is, here it is.
Thank you.

ACKNOWLEDGEMENTS

This book is a journey I started in 2014. I thank those who inspired and mentored me in writing it, both directly and indirectly. I acknowledge my direct mentors: Barry Mitchell, of Uncovering Greatness, and Billy Selekane, CSP, SASHoF, EXPY, who taught me a lot about myself. I learned from some of the best people in their industries, particularly Niel Malan, who taught me to be an Elite Entrepreneur and Digital Marketer Tiger Ninja Level. Robin Banks, who teaches Mind Power, is one of my role models, and I hope to one day take over from him, though he may not know it yet. Coert Coetzee of Wealth Masters taught me to have a long-term view of wealth and legacy, and I am grateful to him.

While writing this book, I had to walk through fire. Literally, Co- bus Visser, of Firewalking Africa, made me walk through fire, and I am proud to be a firewalk instructor. I meet people all the time on my journey who influence me significantly and may not know it. One of them is Brian Walsh, whose platform Real Entrepreneur allowed me to meet most of my mentors and role models.

I have always wanted a life of significance, and, as a result, I learn a lot from many people, too many to mention all of them here. To all of them, I say thank you.

If you can take one thing away from this, get more mentors!

Finally, I would like to acknowledge my mother and older brother, who raised me. My father and brothers, who support me, and my extended family, who believe in me.

WHATS IN IT FOR YOU

- *Description (pain & solution):*

    Why do you wake up every morning to go to work? Will you ever reach the wealth that you dreamed about since you were a child? Do you feel stuck and as though you will never be able to make it? Find a way to live the life you always wanted to live a life which has maximum impact and true, sustainable wealth. Learn the habits of the wealthy and create your ideal future today by changing how you work.

- *Learn How....*

    Your JOB the way you are doing it now may be in the way of your wealth. Wealthy people from all over the world and all walks of life created wealth by changing the way they worked and sometimes where they worked. Make a change immediately and create wealth the same way these ordinary people did.

- *In these pages you will uncover...*

    The secrets of the wealthy which you can use to become wealthy in less time than you ever thought possible

    Learn how to be better at being yourself and make money while doing it.

    How to have a greater impact on yourself and those around you.

- *Write your Benefit Headline:*

  Create Wealth By Changing Your Thoughts and Your Habits or even your JOB!

- *What else will I get from the book?*
  - Identify whether or not you are living the life you want to live.
  - Accept the positive and the negative areas of your life and take responsibility for them.
  - Identify where these areas originate from.
  - Change your thinking with regards with these negative areas.
  - Nurture the positive areas and add some more.
  - Create wealth habits that will guarantee your success.
  - Learn practical ways to create wealth.
  - Learn from masters about protecting your wealth.
  - Create the legacy you want and have dreamed of from your youthful days.
  - Help others to do the same.

TABLE OF CONTENTS

1. Working Your JOB 13
2. What Have You Become? 23
3. You're Creator 32
4. Be Your Own Doctor: Dr. You 47
5. Decisions, Decisions 59
6. The Sales Life 78
7. An Attitude of Gratitude 89
8. Wealthing It 98
9. Journey Wealth 119

CHAPTER 1
WORKING YOUR JOB

Really? You are really reading a book on how to stop working and get wealthy? I'm sorry, but you may need to book a consultation with me, so I can make sure you're okay. Well, now that you have the book, we might as well get started.

As a disclaimer, I will say the following. What you are about to read is not a guarantee for wealth, nor is it a prescription for wealth. Rather, it is advice. It has worked for the people who I learned it from, and it will work for you. Whether or not you use it is your own decision.

My first question to you is a question I asked myself: "Why are you working?" I thought about this question, because I wondered if this working thing is getting me where I want to be. I thought of the long hours I work in the hospital and the stress I go through. I thought of the dreams I had when I was a child and how much greater I thought I would be. The first thought that came into my mind was—would it be possible for me to become wealthy? If so, who in my family was wealthy that I could emulate? I thought of my father, whom I had met at nineteen years of age. His younger brother, my uncle, was, by all accounts, wealthy. He had, however, passed on in a car accident several years ago, long before I questioned the possibility of my being wealthy. This led me to think of a distant relative of my father's family – Billy Selekane. I started reading about him on the Internet and decided that I should learn from him, surely if we were related—even by him sharing the same surname as my father—there was hope.

When I was younger, like most people, I dreamt of who I would become. I dreamt as I ran around the dusty streets of my home township of Katlehong that by age 24, I would be the wealthiest man in the world. I dreamt that I would be voted the most handsome man. Even at the age of five, I thought as I ran, the wind blowing in my face, that I was the fastest boy in the world. What had happened to those dreams of greatness? Had they slowly faded with the sinking 'reality' that life was not easy? Was it the constant reminder by those around me that I had to work for everything? Whatever it was it was so powerful, it had made sure I forgot those young innocent dreams and lived a life prescribed to me by people I don't know, people I would never meet. I ask again, "Why are you working?"

Most people work to make a comfortable living, and understandably so, because these days, you cannot do anything without money. That very statement has been repeated to me by so many people as they justify why they work. I cannot take it away from them, as I have good experience of it myself. The times I have been most stressed were when I didn't have money, money – not a job. Barry Mitchell, of *Uncovering Greatness*, says, "You don't need a JOB to make MONEY". For a long time while working with him, this statement didn't make sense. If not a job, then how else will I make money?

Well, suffice it to say that in this same world we live in, wealthy people are using far more than their jobs to make money. If you can learn what they already know, you, too, can do the same. You can use the resources section of the book to find out more.

For other people, it's more than just making a living for themselves. It's supporting their families, relatives, and other needy people. People use their jobs to put a plate of hot food on the table. They find themselves in these situations, sometimes without choosing. They are the breadwinners and sometimes, they win even less than bread. This is a strong reason to work—when others will suffer if you don't. This type of working is for resilient people who never give up. Unfortunately, while they are working to take care of others, often, there is no one to take care of them. If something does happen to them, those who depend on them suffer even more.

Is there a solution? Perhaps wealth would alleviate this for all involved, but why would one want to be wealthy? How would one achieve this wealth with all the responsibilities they have? These are some of the questions you need to answer if you find yourself in this situation.

Finally, there are those who work to create wealth. They are a different breed of people, admired and despised, envied and disregarded. They are people who, for some reason, became wealthy while the rest of us were slogging away. We see them almost flashing their wealth in our faces. They are relaxing at coffee shops on a Monday morning reading the paper, before driving off in their luxury cars. Who are these people, and how do they create the elusive wealth that they do? Are they living in the same world as the rest of us? Are they operating in a different reality? Whatever the case, we all love to hate them—they are living in a way we only dream about. How do they do it? Well, I decided I would ask them, if not face-to-face, then I would read their books, attend their seminars, and listen to their audio tapes.

It was already clear to me from the time I was studying that the people who are creating wealth are always doing something different. They were not working like most people work, and

because of that, they were getting different results – results they wanted. It led me to question whether my job can put me at risk of not being wealthy. By this time, I was already practicing as a medical doctor. I wasn't even that far into my career, having just completed my community service year. I looked ahead at my seniors and realized they were nowhere near where I wanted to be. Most had lost the passion for what they did and were now doing the job just for the money. It was as though their salary was a puppet master to whose tune they had to dance to. To make it worse, most felt they had no other choice than to keep doing what they do.

Maybe one day, something would change. I learned from them what is embodied in the saying – *If you always do what you always did, you always will get what you always got*. Was I expecting to create wealth that satisfied me by doing what didn't get others before me wealthy? I realized quickly that most of us work at jobs where we are slow to clock in and quick to clock out.

Jobs where we hate the start of the week and love the end of it. Jobs where we are happy at the end of the month and frustrated by the middle of the next month. I realized then that the wealth I wanted was not waiting for me on Monday at work. How could I say this? Am I implying that they weren't paying me well? They were, however, it was according to their terms. I have learned that all salaries will be earned on the employer's terms. All true wealth is earned on the individual's terms. Some may say – *Well, I love my job, and it gives me what I want from it*. That is okay, and I am glad if you are one of those people. My question is, do you want to be wealthy? Why do you want to be wealthy? Can your current job create that wealth for you over the next forty years?

Currently, those who are extremely good at their jobs and are enjoying them may find that their jobs are draining other areas of their wealth. Let me explain it this way: Wealth, according to me, is not only financial. For as many areas of your life as there are, there is wealth in them. I will divide them into two broad groups: internal wealth and external wealth. Internal wealth is spiritual wealth, emotional wealth, and knowledge wealth. External wealth includes family wealth, relationship wealth, and material wealth. There are a lot more categories to be found, and you can tell me about them when you see me.

Work falls under the umbrella of material wealth, because whether it does so successfully or not, it should add to your material wealth. Focusing too much on this category of wealth may hurt all the other groups. However, without this wealth group, all the other groups would suffer, too. The trick is to know which balance works for your particular situation and to make it happen—and soon. Keep in mind that work is not the only way to make money. Coert Coetzee says this, "I have never heard of anyone who worked themselves wealthy." There is a certain attitude to becoming wealthy, and it is the mentality that making money doesn't have to be hard or grueling. It cannot be done alone, and, unlike work, you can never only do it for yourself.

I asked myself if I love what I do for a living. The answer was yes, ever since I can remember, I wanted to be a medical doctor. I wanted to help people get better from their illnesses and, hopefully, help them prevent themselves from being sick in the first place. Maybe I didn't really love the way in which medicine is practiced. The hours are long and tiresome, the pay is reasonable (according to me), but it all relies on me being there. So maybe you don't like what you do for a living at all, however, you ask what else there is to do. You may ask, "How else must I make a living?" "Though I don't like this job, it gives me what I need and provides 'security' and comfort for me and my family."

Perhaps you are one of the few who actually love what they do and could do it at any hour. You need no external motivation or influence. However, you don't make enough material wealth to create the lifestyle you dream of for you and your family. Your family even wonders why you continue doing something that cannot provide for their wishes and desires. Sometimes, it's something that only you can understand. Well, if you have found this job, I would say you are seventy percent of the way there. You should keep at it and try to move closer to the third group of people: the wealthy group– stay focused!

A word on JOB security: it doesn't exist. Your JOB is only as secure as your ability to perform it better than the next person. As secure as your company's ability to stay ahead of the market. As secure as your economy's ability to stay afloat. Those are exactly the kind of dependent thoughts you have about your JOB, which proves that you don't even think it's secure. It's a myth we feed ourselves to mask our hunger for greatness.

These groups of people are as common as a chicken's tooth. I am exaggerating, of course; it does, however, seem like that. They are the group who love what they do and make tons of money doing it. They seem to be able to balance all the wealth groups in their lives. They make this wealth thing look easy and make the rest of us seem like amateurs. This is the group we aim to become like. If we can become like them and do what they do, it is possible to have what they have.

In his book *Start With Why,* Simon Sinek relates that WHY you do what you do is, perhaps, the most important aspect of the whole thing. So powerful that if strong enough, you will outshine all others who do the same thing. So, I ask you – why do you do what you do? Your answer to this question is a very personal one. However, it can only boil down to two things – internal influences and external influences. There are no right or wrong answers, just answers that are holding you back from your dreams and answers that are moving you forward.

Some people do their jobs because they serve a function. They are a means to an end, whatever that end may be. They put food on the table; they provide for our families and give us a sense of purpose. In rare circumstances, those jobs become the lake between us and our wealth. As mentioned before, others relying on your job is a powerful motivator for staying at a job, even if it's draining the life out of you. You often hear parents say to their children, "I have worked my whole life to make sure you guys have a better chance than me..." the end of that sentence is usually encouraging you to do better. Nevertheless, we learn this type of behavior from those around us, particularly those who teach us about money.

We learn to do whatever it takes to never let our loved ones down, and keeping a steady job seems to be high on the list. Perhaps not the jobs, themselves, but what the jobs do for us. They give us status, meaning, and money - money being the most important. Well, perhaps not the money, itself, either. If I were to place one million rand in cash and tell you it's yours on two conditions: you cannot use it and you cannot tell anyone about it, you may tell me to keep it. Well, don't worry; I won't be giving you one million rand. I learned that it is not the money, itself, we want, but what the money can do for us. Understanding this truth changed a lot about how I think of money.

There are those who work systematically to create abundance in all areas of their lives. These are the truly wealthy ones; they are balanced or, rather, balancing, as this is a continuous state of improvement. They are calm in the midst of panic. They have no idea what we mean by month-end blues. They speak about cash flow; they think in the long-term and are constantly looking for more opportunities to create wealth.

As doctors, we focus mostly on the objective aspects of human beings. We examine people's eyesight, but don't ask about their vision. The vision I'm referring to is figurative, like the vision you have about your future. An important question you should ask yourself is, "What is my vision for my life?" This question is so important that the mere asking of it puts you ahead of the crowd. How you get to the answer and how often you review that answer will determine whether your vision will be realized or not.

Let's look at a few examples of how people think about theirvision, in terms of the work they do. Some people's vision is to survive. All they think about is how to breathe the next breath, what their next meal is going to be, and even when the next salary is coming. They have a short-term vision, whether by choice or due to the circumstances they put themselves in or find themselves in. Regardless of which one it is, they feel that jobs, money, and food are scarce, so they need to focus on the now, because life is tough. Just across the residential divide, you find a different group of people. Those who aim to be comfortably comfortable in life and work. This group of people saw the first group and thought, "Well, I'm not going to end up like those guys. I will get a good job, buy a nice house and car, and live comfortably. I don't want too much, just a little more than enough." They are able to focus not only on themselves, but the extended family as well, in a comfortable way. These people are often mistaken for the wealthy, because their comforts are mostly flashy and visible. Their vision is largely mid-term with fewer long-term goals.

In contrast to both groups, the wealthy manage all the parts of their vision with the greatest clarity. They have a systemized vision—one that covers all the areas of their lives (fig. 1.1). It is no coincidence that figure 1.1 resembles a ship's wheel – don't give responsibility for navigating your wealth to other people. You are the captain of your own wealth ship. The wealthy have a legacy-based long-term vision that will likely outlive them, sometimes spanning 200 to 300 years. This informs their mid- term vision, which, in turn, dictates what they do in the short-term. All these flow into each other, as does a left turn during a well-planned journey from Johannesburg to Durban in South Africa. Each turn, rest stop, or ramp is a seemingly small, but very important, part of the greater journey.

Back to main road, they realize the link between the choices they make every day and their end goal. This is true vision; it is far more than the ability to see or the ability to plan. It concerns not only

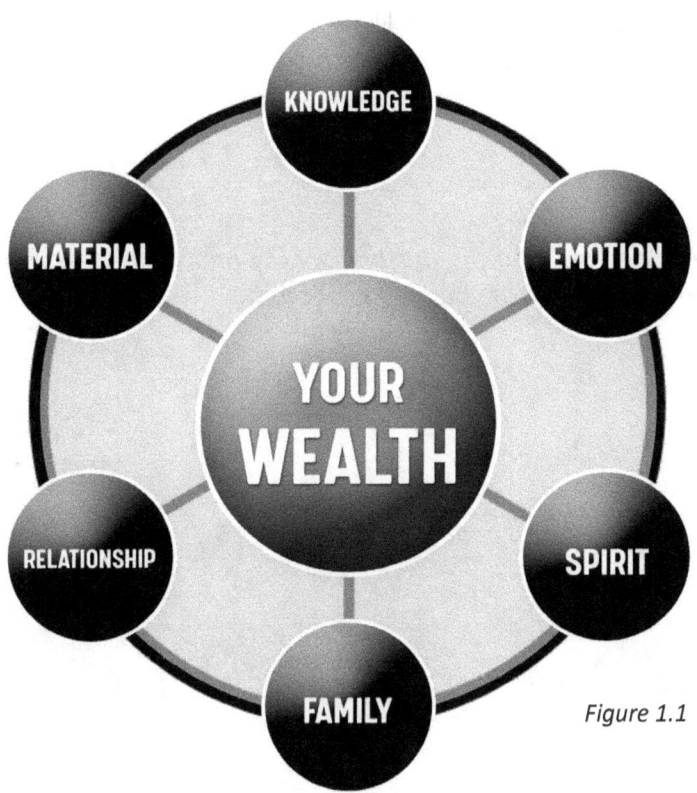

Figure 1.1

you or your family, but your community, suburb, village, province, country, continent, and even the globe. Some people have a vision that covers the universe, because they realize the actions they take today may someday have an impact on the universe.

Your vision in life is closely linked to your goal. In my view, the one dictates the contents of the other. In other words, your vision must dictate your actions. Your 'why' must dictate your how. If not in this order, it becomes difficult to understand how the small things fit into the big picture. It makes burnout much more likely, and makes even the most enjoyable task feel like a mundane job. Think about all these declarations as we continue our journey ensuring that our jobs never stop us from becoming wealthy.

Up Next

Let's explore the idea of your being; why and how its determining your wealth and what you can do about it.

CHAPTER 2
WHAT HAVE YOU BECOME?

There is something you need to think about. It may sound cliché and overdone, but what is your goal in your life? Before answering this question, understand the following. *Who* dictates what your goal is? *When* did you start having these goals? Are they static or changing? Are you keeping track of your progress?

Perhaps your goal is to be a good person; after all you take nothing else with you to the afterlife. Whatever your spiritual inclination, most people think very deeply about what kind of person they have become and are becoming.

What is a good person? Good for who?

By whose standards?

Will being a good person serve your values?

In most cases, a good person is a comparison to another person. I have learned that you should always make this 'other person' your old self, strive to be better than you used to be. If you compare yourself to others, you go down a slippery slope. In other cases, people seem to choose either being a good person OR a wealthy person. In their minds, the two cannot coexist in one person; however, the answer is both, as T. Harv Eker puts it. I have been taught the same in wealth – make sure you seek and work for wealth that is wealth **to you**. Have your cake and eat it, too.

Some people seek only to have loads of money. They dream of all the things they could do to get some of this money. Apart from the readers of this book, others even think of the lottery, crime, quick fixes, and other futile ways to try to create wealth. It's not that you cannot win the lottery, but, as Chris Hock puts it, "The lottery is punishment for those who don't understand mathematics." You could win, of course, but until then, you will always lose. And, sometimes, even when you win, you still lose. I have found that money, in and of itself, is of no use to you. As mentioned earlier, it is what the money does for you that is what you seek. Find out first what you desire the money for; be very specific as to your requirements, and, then, the plan for making the money will come.

Whether you want to be a good person or have loads of money understand this: the answer is both. You can exist as a human being on planet earth who is a good person and also a wealthy person. If you don't strive for a life in which you accept that both can coexist, the two will always be in conflict in your mind.

When you start thinking about being a good person, your mind will justify your financial poverty. When you start getting more and more financially free, your brain will oppose this, because you are becoming a 'bad person'. Then, it's just a matter of time before you have sabotaged your finances and are back at a place you don't like. This is just one example of the mutual exclusivity we create between financial wealth and other forms of wealth we desire in our lives. For as long as you believe that when you have wealth you cannot have something else, that will remain true for you forever.

Begin today to write down all the things you falsely believe you can't be, do, or have when you have wealth. Start to write that you can and will have wealth and be a good person. Continue doing the same for all these 'beliefs' and put this list in a place where you can read it every day.

One of the things we ask the least about ourselves is, "Who am I?" We are quick to ask others this question, though we don't fully understand ourselves. Who are you? Are you the product of your parents? Fifty-fifty, or sixty-forty? Are you a product of your environment and the people around you, or are you self-determined and not affected by your circumstances? I have found that we live our lives mostly not as ourselves, but as the people we want others to see. To answer the question above, we are all those things, having been influenced by our family, friends, and community. We are molded by our environment, circumstances, and life experiences. In all this having *chosen* how these things will affect us. We choose to become the people we become. No one, no matter what they do, can force us to become something else. They may delay you, they may derail you, they may even help you decide what you **don't want to be,** but no matter how long it takes, you will get back on those rails and reach the destination you have chosen.

Having asked yourself the question "Who am I?" You should decide to take the journey to finding out. This is the most important journey you will ever take in your life. It is during the journey that we find out who we need to become, so we can truly enjoy our destination. Remember that what we call a journey is also a destination. Make sure you enjoy it.

No matter how you get there, ensure that you decide to go and travel the whole way. A lonesome valley, some might say. It is the only journey that no one can take with you or for you. If you decide never to take it, it will remain thus for eternity. You may ask how to take this journey, where you should start. Well, lucky for you and me, there are people who, like travel agents, can help you find the best means of getting there. Once you understand who you want to be, you can easily find these people.

You are literally one in seven billion and counting. You are becoming more and more unique by the minute. Yet, most of us spend our lives wanting to be other people, doing what those people love doing and having what they have. This is sad and, unfortunately, we cannot escape this desire, unless we have a true sense of who we are. In the absence of the real you, your brain will latch on to the most desirable 'other' people it can find. It will make you find pleasure in imitating them and later chastise you for doing it. What a travesty that some people will leave earth without ever giving us the pleasure of meeting them. Instead, they will make popular the people they are imitating who are, themselves, imitating others.

Having found the true you and your purpose - you must discover what you think, say, and do most often, because it is shaping who you are becoming. What this means is, in addition to your past experiences, which have shaped what you think of yourself, this is what you think about every day. These thoughts affect how you feel and, in turn, what you do. Finally, this produces the results you have in your life. Find out what results you are getting in all the areas of your potential wealth (fig. 2.1).

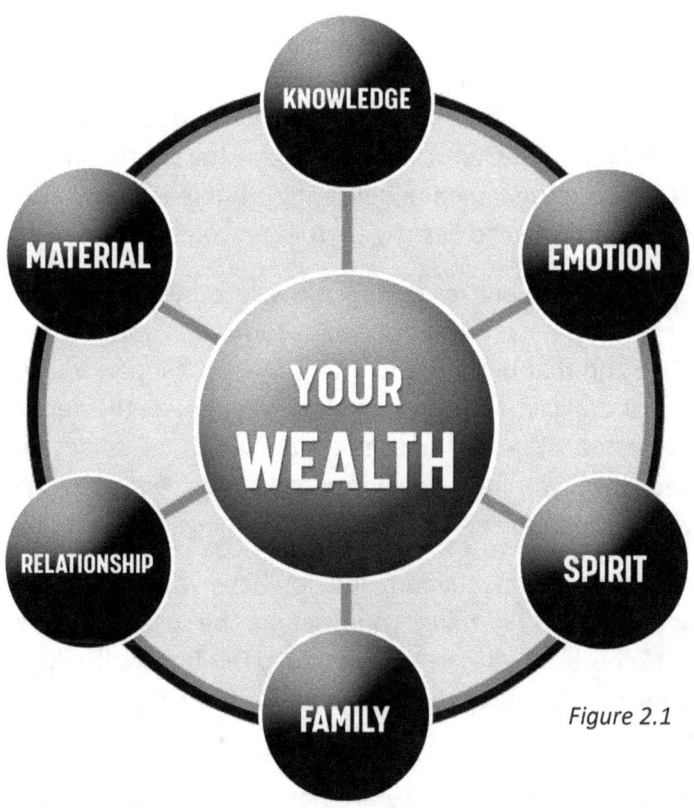

Figure 2.1

Decide whether you like these results or dislike them, whether they are moving you forward or pushing you back. Now, find the ones which you like and are proud of. Congratulate yourself for having made them happen; they are also there because of you. Look at the ones that are not perfect yet, and accept that you are responsible for them being there. Do not lay the blame on anyone else, even if it's tempting or justifiable in some sense to do so. Resolve to **make** them in the way that they need to be, then, **act** as quick as lightning. Even as you start asking the questions in the right way, the place where you look for answers will be more appropriate.

Some people look at these imperfect results in their lives and hope that the breakthrough will come someday. The breakthrough is already there with you. If you want to see it, go to the mirror *alone*. Say to the person on the other side, "I'm ready for my breakthrough now. We can go ahead." Repeat this until you are certain the person in the mirror understands. The fundamental belief at play here is that you have the power to both create and destroy anything in your life.

Some speak of fate and coincidence, while others speak of destiny. Speak of whatever you want, but decide today that you are the creator of that fate and that destiny, and that it will not happen coincidentally in your favor or against you. It is and has always been the person in the mirror using the influences of the outside world. Yes, things may have happened which you have no control over, however, you reacted, and whatever you continue to think about those things is all up to you.

You have your current situation, and you have your future aspirations and what you want. The things you want may be so huge and scary that you don't know how you can achieve them. This book will help with that in some ways, but only as much as you want it to. If you plan to eat an elephant, do it the only way possible – one piece at a time.

The things you want to achieve are not events but journeys that you embark on. Here is an example; you find a beautiful field on which you would like to build your dream house. When are you wealthy? Is it the day you have finished building the house and are living in it? Or is it the day you make a firm decision, feel the joy of the decision, and start taking the first action on building the house? If you don't enjoy the journey, you may wait a long time for your joy to come. Finally, when you get to the finished house, you may find it not as joyous as you thought. Life is a journey of smaller journeys. It begins in a journey and ends in a journey. Open your heart and mind—make it an extraordinary journey!

Tony Robbins speaks of reaching the end of your goal and still feeling unsatisfied, making you wonder what the point of it all was. Whenever you encounter a problem, use your own mind to overcome the problem first, then, physically overcome it. Everything made by man started as an intangible thing, a thought. Then, it was spoken of and planned. Finally, action was taken to bring it to existence.

So, who creates the results in your life? We have briefly mentioned this concept: your thoughts determine your feelings, which, in turn, determine your actions and translate to your results. See fig 2.2, which represents a film reel. Like a movie creator, you are responsible for deciding which part of the film you cut off and which parts you leave in to create your life movie.

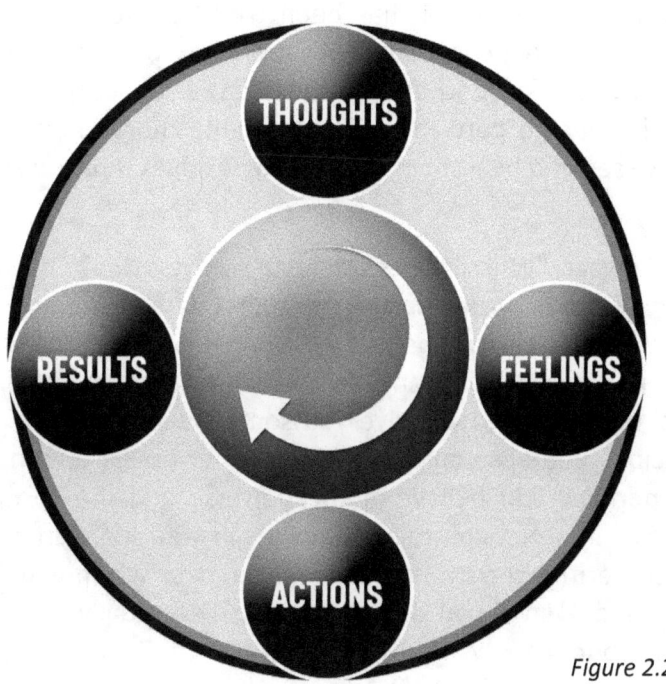

Figure 2.2

Some of us live our lives like the banks – there's a permanent sign on our "window" that says, "The keys to the safe are held by an external security company," as though someone must come to create the results in your life. Throughout all the seminars I attended, I realized that all the best motivators and trainers in the world are only able to guide you up to the level of feelings. From there, the ball is in your court.

In the same way, a doctor can only explain your illness, the treatment, and how the treatment is going to help you. You really cannot expect them to consume the tablets that are going to make you feel better. Sometimes, I feel that this is our expectation of motivational speakers and trainers, teachers, and governments.

Some may say motivation has been tried and tested and found wanting. The reality is that motivation has been tested, found challenging, and left untried. It is much easier to accept what most others do. Due to herd mentality, we unite more about negative things we see and hear more often than positives. Are you surprised by that?

I will ask again, "Who creates the results in your life?" It's not that there is a right or wrong answer, only that whatever you believe is the answer remains the answer until you change it. It's not so much a right or wrong answer than an answer that causes you to progress, regress, or stagnate. I will give you some clues as to who may be responsible. Perhaps you believe in a higher power and intelligent being, perhaps you believe in the universe and the cosmos and that those are what controls the results in your life. Perhaps there is a predetermined path laid out for you, over which you have no control, and even if you deviate, you will eventually find yourself back on your path. Whichever it is, does this not remove some responsibility from yourself? After all, the same intelligent being is there for everyone else around you, but some are doing better than you and some worse.

Sometimes, the people around us seem to help us produce brilliant results, but when they are not around, what happens? Some people seem to drain the energy out of us; things work better as long as they are not around. Whatever the case maybe, ask yourself if other people are responsible for the results you are getting in your life. Perhaps your breakthrough will come when someone from somewhere comes and does something. You hold on to this hope, as your dreams, desires, and wants wait along with you at the bus stop of hope, while others are drenching themselves in the rain of opportunity. I'm not saying that you won't reach a tentative stage in your life when you don't know if you are coming or going. I am saying that while you are at the bus stop of hope, use the panels to build yourself a go-kart, and begin your journey to your next journey. What I mean by that is, you **create** your own results. I have said this before, but it takes time to sink in, because it is not a natural thought.

Up Next

Not all journeys are the same. They are neither good nor bad, but all inevitably lead to another journey. Learn to enjoy each and every one of them. If anything, at least learn from all of them. How? By creating the journey and not only accepting the road signs as the appear. You are the creator.

I will suggest that in life, you are not searching for a destina- tion. Rather, you are searching for your Journey of Journeys: the journey that will lead you to the place of ultimate wealth. As soon as you think you have arrived, you are at the beginning of another journey.

CHAPTER 3
YOU'RE CREATOR

My mission statement in life is this:

> *I help people be better at being themselves,
> by awakening the creator within them.*

This is the answer I give people who as me what I do. Some find this fascinating, while others...let's just say they ask if I understood the question. Why is this my mission?

I have decided it is. It is why I am here. Where?

In this universe.

We have too many people who will never grace this earth, not as themselves, anyway. Some of them are reading this book—no, not you, others somewhere else. I would love to meet you, but if I never do, promise that wherever you are, you are truly you. When you are you, you can bring to the world the unique gift that only you can. You can succeed in the way you want to. People who succeed take the creation of their life results as their responsibility.

The best way to predict the future is to create it
- Peter Drucker.

Others are there to help us or watch us; some may even try to impede us. In the end, they are still not responsible for the results we get. They build go-karts from the bus stop materials, and you see them whizzing past in life. They believe that everything they need is with them.

All I need is within me now!
- Robin Banks

They believe that all the tools needed to achieve and solve everything are in their surroundings.

Everything is in the room
- Barry Mitchell.

How do these people do this and how can we do the same and even more?

Do What You Love
- Song by The Muffinz.

Do: Passion

You have heard many people say, "You should do what you love, what you are passionate about. Then, you will make money." That may be easier said than done. The pursuit of what one loves is as old as the search for the meaning of life. In fact, one may say the two are inseparable, both having boggled the minds of men for centuries. Let us assume, however, you are able to use the resources I recommend in order to discover your passion and use it to create your wealth in a good balance. Is it possible for this passion to burn you out?

Some may find that as they are looking for their passion, it seems more and more like hard work. They may complain about the difficulty of it all and decide to do something different. You see a lot among students of this in higher education institutions. Each year, the pursue a different course of study, because the previous course was either too boring, too difficult, or just not for them. The issue here, of course, was never the course, but the student and his passions. Too few of us find what makes us alive and excited in terms of work and purpose. We mill through boring lectures, boring jobs, and live boring lives, all in the hope of retiring happily.

If you don't enjoy the journey, it is unlikely you will enjoy the destination. This is because the journey and the destination are a unit. They may appear different. They behave like breathing – you cannot love inhaling and hate and exhaling, if you want to live. In wealth creation, you cannot love the destination while hating the journey.

Therefore, doing what you love cannot burn you out, as long as you are also being who you love to be. The suggested best person to be is yourself – that elusive being who buries his head in the deep recesses of your mind, afraid they might not be accepted by others. This person is scary, because they are like a figure in the night. You see them in an alley, and you cannot comprehend what he might do next.

In one of Dr. John Demartini's talks on values, he expressed that if you need vacations to give you a break from what you do, you have not yet found your passion. This is because what you are passionate about does not tire you out. In fact, others may need to ask you if you don't feel tired, and you will be shocked by such a question. With this, doing what you truly love should not get to the point of being harmful to your body or being, either you get stronger and smarter, or you deliberately make it work in a balanced way. Whichever way, remember that it's *both* wealth and family time; wealth and spirituality, not an 'either or' situation. You need to *create* it that way. Certain people have become so connected with their passion that they can do it even in their sleep. You may wonder how. They do this by leveraging the time they have—twenty-four hours—and using a team to increase their productivity.

If, as a doctor, you can only see four patients in an hour, how do you leverage your time? You build a team of ten doctors who can now see four patients of their own in the same hour. You have now effectively seen forty patients in an hour. This is true wealth: the power to leverage your time by utilizing the time of others. This is how you could be 'doing' what you love, even in your sleep. Collaboration is the ultimate tool in fighting burnout.

Do: Money

Too many people spend money they earned...to buy things they don't want...to impress people that don't like.
– Will Rogers

Is money even real? I have often thought of this question, which has plagued the minds of men since the beginning of time. I have wondered why money seems to have a mind of its own, seeming to choose whom it spends the most time with and making the rest enjoy just spending it. It has resulted in joy and tragedy; in love and hate; in peace and war. It has been used to change the world, while making it stay the same. It has been used to progress the human race and also fix matches, all for the purpose of some unknown goal conceived in the minds of men. Money doesn't exist. I will say it again: money doesn't exist! Having said this, I want a lot of it.

The Bible states, "The love of money is the root of all evil." Over the years, this has been paraphrased as, "Money is the root of all evil," a statement with a completely different meaning. A statement that has grieved many into living an austere existence, sometimes to their own family's detriment. I believe that money, itself, is as evil as the air we breathe, meaning that people with evil hearts breathe the same air as those with good hearts, but they do different things with it. Money, itself, does not do evil; people who possess it do. Money, itself, never did a single good deed, but people who had it did. Both groups of people still exist and will continue to exist as long as humans exist.

As mentioned before, I don't believe people love money, itself. This is because money, itself, can do nothing. If you were the first or last human alive, money would have absolutely no meaning or use to you. However, add a couple billion more people, a systemized currency system based on bartering and exchange of value and – boom! This is a rudimentary explanation of this complex system, but it will suffice for our purposes.

Money exists now in the time you live in, whether in physical, electronic, or blockchain form. For the most part, you will need it to create your vision and achieve your goals. You cannot wish it away, and you cannot destroy it. Like the human race, money adapts to the world it finds itself in. It lives in the minds of men, whether wealthy or poor, Christian or Muslim, white or black, and everyone in between.

Destroy the idea from your mind that money comes with evil. Replace it, instead, with the truth that money magnifies your heart and mind. If your heart is full of evil, money will just make it easier and allow a larger scale of evil. If, however, in your heart lies good, money will make that good grow in the most amazing way ever. Therefore, don't think you can remain good by having less money; become good by doing more good and need more money for more good. This is the true power of money: it is a magnifier.

Perhaps you are from the school of thought that says money can't buy happiness. Well, can poverty? Money cannot buy love, either, but hasn't poverty has frustrated even the most resilient love many a time? More and more today, people are fighting, filing for divorce, and separating because of money. Does more money bring more problems? Perhaps, but does being poor take away problems? Would you rather deal with your problems in poverty, or drive to them in style? Whatever the case may be – make a decision, and live with that decision. You can change it when you feel it no longer serves you. It is neither right, nor wrong; it just pushes you forward to your vision or pulls you back. Once your decision is made, do not complain or worry, and don't regret it. Rather, make another decision and take the action that will satisfy your desire.

Money magnifies your heart; I have heard this repeated over and over by one of my mentors, Barry Mitchell, as he strives to teach all his students. He finally broke through to me, and from that day forth, I decided that I was wealthy and will forever be, not on anyone's terms but my own. I will leave a legacy—a great one—and no one can stop me, except me. I resolved not to stop myself. I decided what matters to me most in life and made a plan of how I would create the world I desire for those people. If I don't like something, I will create it in the way I like it. If I feel something can be done better, I will not hesitate to make it happen. I will ensure that whomever I meet receives more value than they can ever fathom. I resolved that this is the greatest calling for my life.

Do: You

I am a billionaire, with or without papers and numbers on any screens. I now believe this fully, and daily am becoming that person. I learn what people like myself do, and do these things. I learn to speak the way they do, and think the same things.

I know that, come what may, I will soon enough have what they have, and I will enjoy the journey leading there. I am not telling you this to boast. I am saying this to the part in me that thinks I can never be wealthy, that little voice that creeps in once in a while, teasing and taunting me about my current 'reality'. This is the self I am competing with daily, the me who tries to stop me from the inevitable greatness for which I was created. It is the equivalent of your own self that is asking you right now why you have the audacity to *think* you could be wealthy, let alone actually become wealthy. It is your mind, your most powerful tool. It can raise you up or send you crashing down, depending on how you learn to control it.

Make it your number one goal in life to learn how your own mind works, and you will be far ahead of 99 percent of the world. Then, make it a point to find your values and your purpose, for these dictate your day-to-day existence. Then, start on your journey correctly and consistently on the path to success. Here is an example: you have your vision (discussed above), which is like your destination. Learning how your mind works, your value, and your purpose, is like finding out what kind of transportation you are. Perhaps a bicycle, perhaps a car, a train, or even an airplane. Whatever the case may be, this initial step will ensure that you know how you get to the destination. If you are an airplane that thinks it's a bicycle, you will always be looking for your handle bars and pedals, instead of looking for the cockpit. As a result, you can never move, and even bicycles who know they are bicycles will complete their journey before you move an inch.

Once you know who and what you are, accept it or change it. Take action, as this is the only way to affect the physical world. Having done this, plan your route to the destination. This is setting your goals and planning their execution. Having made it clear in your mind, take action on those goals. If you don't know how, learn either by listening first, then doing, doing first, then listening, or a combination of the two. Just take action. While taking action, you will find that there is that thing you are most passionate about.

Make it clear in your mind why you are passionate, and resolve to do that in the greatest way you ever can. Use that passion to serve as many people as possible, and if you are adding value to their lives, you will start to deserve value back in your life.

Billy Selekane and James McNeil have spoken about using your purpose in life to serve others, and both have courses to help you discover how to do exactly that. This brought me to a strange question: why are our passions not being sought from the time we are young? Dr. Demartini believes that these values can be found quite early on in adolescence, and young people may begin pursuing these passions from then on. What a world that would be, a place where people do things they are good at, because they are really passionate about them. A world full of energy being used for the right reasons, an ideal world. I hear you saying, "Well, we are in the real world, where we have to pay bills." This is true, just remember this the next time you are standing in a queue to pay some mundane bill – you are not here to just pay bills. Everyone has bills, however, bills are only a byproduct of existence on earth and should never cloud the bigger picture. If we have the pleasure to meet one day after you have read this book and you tell me about 'paying the bills' as the reason why you are stuck, don't be surprised if I take a moment of silence and remember all the other heroes who are famous for having paid all their bills.

Do: De-Serve

> *You will get all you want in life, if you help enough other people get what they want.*
> – Zig Ziglar

Serve first, give other people what they want, and you will get what you want. This is a lesson in reciprocity, a lesson in Ubuntu (the African principle) –this world demands that we serve one another. At the time of going to print, McDonald's was said to be the largest fast food outlet in the world *serving* over seventy million people per day worldwide. You may say what you want about their business or their practices; they are *serving* people, and, in turn, they deserve the money they receive.

Learn to serve, put yourself second just for once today, and find ten people to serve without expecting anything in return. Write down the events that followed, and send them to us. Inevitably, you will find that you got more things you wanted during that time, you felt more fulfilled, and more opportunities opened up that you would not have received otherwise.

Learn to serve not only others, but yourself, too. You should be very important to yourself—not vain, but important. Treat yourself as such, and others will do the same. Your perception about yourself is your reality. You deserve the wealth you have now and more. You deserve the wealth you are yet to receive.

Just one question: how many people are you willing to serve? That number will determine how much you deserve.

Do: Balance

You need a balanced life; a work-life balance. You need a balance of business and pleasure. What balance? Who decided that? According to whom must these things be balanced? I am not saying they shouldn't be; I am merely making sure you question why you think that. Resolve now to not do anything you don't know the reason for, no matter how trivial. This is because it is a dangerous existence to be in. You may as well eat broken glass, because celebrities think it's cool. Many of us desire wealth or money, because other people respect wealthy people, not because we have a vision of what this wealth will do for us or others. We then degenerate our morals and standards to the point of doing anything to acquire money in large amounts. This is not wealth, because it doesn't serve others. Rather, it hurts and denigrates them.

As a result, it will not be sustainable. If it is not sustainable, how will it leave a legacy? Consider that as you think of that deal you are about to get into.

The balances we seek are both desired and created by us. How we desire them is through our upbringing and the environment we grew up in. We then create the circumstances within which they must exist. Let's assume you decide that your work-life balance will be 30:70—in other words you will spend thirty percent of your time working and seventy doing whatever you consider life. Depending on how strong this desire is and how concretely you create it in your mind, you may be able to achieve it. What happens, however, when a family member falls ill and you now need to spend more time in the life portion? Will your mind accept this, or will it start to beat you up about it?

If, for whatever reason, you need to work more, again your mind punishes you about it, until such a point as you decide that maybe it doesn't matter, and you forget about the balance you just created. So, I ask you again, what balance? Who created it? Why is it there? The question is not whether it is right or wrong—it is whether it's pushing you toward your vision or pulling you away. It may be your spiritual and your financial life; it may be relationships and work. Decide today that you will have a balance that works perfectly and, then, set out to create that balance.

All the things in your body that balance themselves out, like your blood pressure and your heart rate, do so by 'knowing' three simple things: how they want things to be, what they are now, and how to change them.

In your life, too, there are feedback loops you need to use to make sure you are on the correct path for. For you, we will add two more. These five simple steps are questioning that Tony Robbins uses as part of his problem-solving question list in his book *Awaken the Giant Within:*

1. *What is great about this problem/situation/challenge?*
2. *What is not perfect yet?*
3. *What am I willing to do to make it the way I want it?*
4. *What am I willing to no longer do in order to make it the way I want it?*
5. *How can I enjoy the process while I do what is necessary to make it the way I want it?*

I, myself, have used this same technique whenever I am faced with challenges, and I have been surprised how well it has worked. Try it for a week with everything you experience that you think is a challenge.

Do: Time

The biggest challenge we face in the working environment is trading time for money—to be more specific, trading life for money. This is the paradox in the typical job scenario – when you have a lot of time, it's likely you don't have a lot of money to spend during that time. When you finally have enough money, it's likely that you don't have enough time in which to spend it.

I realized this as a medical student: we would have at least a month holiday between semesters, and I would wish I could use that time to travel the world. When I finally graduated and started earning a salary, I could afford to travel, but only had two weeks leave, which were dictated by my employer. This caused a yearning in my heart to one day take control of my time and, therefore, of my life. This would not be for my sake only, but for the sake of my current and future families.

There is a joke that says doctors are the people who leave home before the children are awake and arrive home after the children are asleep and use money to make up for the lost time. I thought about this, and it's not really a joke, nor is it only doctors who experience this. This is the saddest thing you can do to yourself and your family.

My mother was the kind of person who worked hard to get herself out of poverty. Having been raised in rural Transkei, she had to educate herself and work in order to change her destiny. She decided that her children would not go through what she went through, and, indeed, she ensured we got a better education than we would otherwise get if we were raised in the rural areas. I started to feel that I owe it to myself first to be wealthy; secondly, I owe it to my mother, who sacrificed her youth to make a better life for me. Thirdly, I owe it to my future family, who will want to spend time with me, since I'm such an awesome person. I promised myself this after seeing how people still do things, like my mother, who was born in 1950 and is still working today. I believe that working hard is very important, but it has hardly made anyone wealthy. Perhaps they were raised to think that this is the only way to survive. I would like to believe that this is an important quality to have, if it results in wealth. If not, it alienates you from yourself and from your loved ones.

Some say, "Well, being lazy doesn't pay the bills." This is where the clichéd but true saying comes in: work smart, not hard. No one will just give you money, that is true, but you can exchange money for value. Your 'job' is to know and understand your true value, and serve others with it, so they can give you money for it. Replace money in the previous sentence with whatever it is you consider wealth. How will they know your true value? You have to know it first, and, then, be able to sell it, communicate it, and put it across. Call it what you want, this is the sequence it goes in. If, however, you decide that people will sense it telepathically, you may struggle for eternity.

Do: Work

(It's okay at this point to re-read the title of the book in disbelief.)

Almost all worthwhile things in life require work to be put into them. I'm not here to encourage you to stop working! I'm here to point out to you that you do need to work, but with the end goal of becoming very, very wealthy. To do so, you need to realize that initially, you may work for money, but, eventually, money needs to work for you. If you do not keep this in mind from the time you are in school, you will forever work for money, trading your life in units of time. How enjoyable it is to be in control of your time and your life; to not worry about the next meal, but, rather, to worry that you may have too many meals and can give some away.

How enjoyable to not worry that you can't give toward your charitable organizations, but to worry that you are giving too much. These are what Neil Malan of Elite, Inc. calls luxury problems. Problems like having too many clients and too much business. This is the point you should be striving for.

Begin with the end in mind. Write down now five things that you want to have achieved by the time you finish this book. Make them measurable goals you strongly desire, and ensure you mean them. Then, show the written-down goals to someone else, someone who can keep you accountable. Review these when you get halfway through the book and, then, again at the end of the book.

In order to know the end, the destination, we need to know where we are. Where are you in your life? Perhaps you are young, you have time, and can afford to make many mistakes yet. Perhaps this is true. On the other hand, perhaps you have matured in years and are in your mid-adult life, and you feel there are so many things you need to do, but you don't know if you will ever get to them. Your life now pretty much dictates who you are. The final group is the elderly, those whom people think of when wisdom is mentioned. Perhaps you fall under this group; what more can be done for you? They say you are at the end of your mortal coil.

Whichever group you fall under, it is never too late to seek your true wealth. Yes, your true wealth, the wealth you consider wealth. The wealth you always dreamed of and still do sometimes. Where are you right now in terms of achieving that wealth? Ask yourself that, and ask a close friend or relative. Write the response down in two parts: the first is the positive achievements you consider to be moving you toward your wealth. Secondly, write down all the negative things you feel are holding you back from your true wealth. Having done this, ensure you add daily to the first list by doing more things that add to your wealth than things that take away from it. This is a modification on Brian Tracy's process when he speaks of the *21 Irrefutable Laws of Money*.

Know where you are going. You have a list of five things you want to achieve before finishing this book. This is your destination in the very short term. Write down the vision you have for the end of your life in terms of the wealth areas (fig. 1.1). Write a minimum of three per area. What three things will you be, do, or have when you have spiritual wealth? An example is you would be a better human being, you would do a daily good deed, and you would have self-contentment. Your responses should be what you consider to be wealth in those areas of your life. There is no wrong or right answer. After finishing this exercise, decide that you will have these goals in your lifetime. Read *Think and Grow Rich* by Napoleon Hill, if you haven't already. Read it again if you have.

Finally, always check if you are on track with these goals and find a way to be accountable to them. A good way is to either find an accountability partner who understands your path and also wants to achieve greatness in life, or find a mentor who has achieved what you desire to achieve, at least in some way. Arrange regular meetings with such mentors or peers, in order to review your progress. This step, alone, will separate you from being a potential success to being an actual success.

The above has been an introduction to the journey we will travel together. We will meet many challenges and experience many joys during our journey. Remember this: all my teachers and I can only guide you through this journey; you will have to walk it on your own.

The journey of a thousand miles begins with the first step
- Confucius

Up Next

I will show you how you can be the 'doctor' of your wealth in your life. I will give you a concept that will teach you a little about medicine and a little about your wealth.

Disclaimer: The 'doctor' referred to above is by no means the academic qualification conferred by accredited higher education institutions, but, rather, a conceptual idea relating to the functions of a doctor when it comes to wealth. You may not call yourself a doctor hereafter, because of the above paragraph or the chapter to follow. Always seek appropriate medical expertise for medical conditions.

Now that the fine print is out of the way, let's go.

CHAPTER 4
BE YOUR OWN DOCTOR: DR. YOU

In many medical resuscitation programs, particularly the ones provided by the American Heart Association, the training for the emergency that happens in the hospital is quite systematic.

If someone collapses at home, the sequence of events will likely be less systematic than if the same person collapses in a hospital. This is because you, at home, are not likely to deal with emergencies that often, unless you are in the medical or paramedical professions; whereas, a hospital is a place where dealing with this is very well a requirement.

The system looks at a few things. Without starting an emergency resuscitation guideline, I will give you the gist of it, so that you will understand the concepts. This does not qualify you to perform any resuscitation on a person—there are training facilities for that.

The scenario is that someone collapses in front of you, and you don't know what's wrong with them. I will explain briefly what you would do for each, so that you can understand the differences between the different situations.

Situation 1 – You are the only one there.

- After trying to wake him up by tapping his shoulder and calling for help
- You would check his pulse.
- If you couldn't feel it you would start compressions on their chest. If you have never been trained in resuscitation you would continue these compressions until help arrives.
- If you had been trained, then you would alternate the compressions with making sure that the airway is open and giving breaths to the person at certain intervals and checking the pulse after those intervals.
- This is better than nothing but still not the ideal situation to have for the person who collapsed. Say another person comes.

Situation 2 – There are two of you.

When the second person arrives, and they have called the ambulance:

- They would be responsible for giving breaths while you give the compressions.
- But because compressions done correctly are so tiring you would swap out with him at two minute intervals.
- You would then be taking care of giving the person breaths but also encouraging the person giving compressions to do

it well. You would tell him if he is not fast enough, if he is not doing it hard enough you would make sure he doesn't interrupt the flow of the compressions.

- This situation is better for the person who collapsed than the first one. But say now the person was in a hospital.

Situation 3 – *You are in the hospital emergency room.*

In this situation, the person walked in to the emergency room and, then, collapsed. There are seven emergency-trained personnel, including an experienced emergency doctor.

Whoever finds the patient first would tap the patient's shoulder, calling his name. If he doesn't respond, a code is called.

- This means that the team that resuscitates is called. While others are on their way, the first person checks the pulse very quickly, and if he can't find it – he starts compressions.

- The other staff arrive and immediately take on the necessary roles and have the required equipment in good working order.

1. *Circulation* – This is the person already compressing the chest.

2. *Airway* – This person makes sure the airway remains open by placing the patient in the proper position. They may also be required to put in tubes that will keep the airway open.

3. *Breathing* – This person makes sure that the patient gets breaths when the person compressing gives them the interval to do so. They may use a bag-mask device, also called an *Ambu-Bag*™.

4. *Defibrillator* – This person makes sure that the machine available and will connect it to the patient, in anticipation of such a need.

5. *Drugs* – This person will prepare the drugs or medicines used in an emergency and record when what was given.

6. *Time keeper* – This person will record the time and alert the team at certain intervals how much time has passed since the resuscitation was started and how much time since any drugs were given.

7. The last person is the *most experienced* emergency staff member – in this situation, the emergency doctor. You would think his role would be one of the above running around doing this and that. His role, however, is to lead the team and determine the direction of the resuscitation. He would not compress or give breaths or anything else. Instead, he would be thinking critically on what kind of patient this is, why he collapsed, and how to get him stabilized in the shortest possible time. Most likely by reversing whatever caused the collapse, if possible.

This situation is the best that a patient can have and is likely to have the best outcomes, too.

How does this apply to you and your wealth? Well, the three scenarios are an analogy to any area you would like to create wealth. Consider as an example your financial situation as the patient. When alone and well trained, you can resuscitate this patient to a certain level, but soon—if doing it properly – you will get very tired. So, although it can work, it doesn't give much time for the patient to respond, because you, the rescuer, are tired.

This is much the same as trying to get your financial situation to another level – from work to wealth, if you will. Alone, it is theoretically possible. However, with help, it is assured it is only a matter of your thoughts and the time and effort you put into making it happen.

This may sound vague, but consider it again and again before taking on a new project. Ask yourself whether it will succeed better if you go it alone, or if you have assistance. The answer you arrive to is neither right nor wrong – just ensure it is the best answer for you.

If you have a business, consider the scenario above as a situation where you must take your business to the next level of life. Here the role-players above would be defined as below:

- The model/concept, itself, is like your business plan, your business proposal, your investment plan. It guides your actions in a very specific way.

- Circulation, airway, and breathing as critical processes or resources without which your business cannot survive. Cashflow, sales and customers, products, and services. These are all things which I consider critical.

- 'Disability', which assesses your strategy, capacity of Operation, and the balance of income and expenditure. This includes the service providers who help you assess these. legal, accounting, and finance. It also correlates with proper business practices, which can all adversely affect your ability to operate. This may be overlooked if your only focus is on the category above.

- Defibrillator – I consider this to be an injection of value into your business. This can either be in the form of investment or, more importantly, the time and skills of a business mentor. However, avoid keeping a mentor as back-up. I will share where on this framework the mentor must be. Though a defibrillator may not be used in all medical scenario, its presence is compulsory, because when the occasion does arise for its use, it saves lives.

- Timekeeper – Inside your business, these are the numbers. Bank statements, balance sheets, income statements, etc. that you get from service providers. Outside your business, these are all the regulatory bodies that allow your business to exist, if you comply with the laws. They cannot sell for you, give you money, or run your business, they reflect in a 2D format what is happening in your business.

- The experienced emergency staff member – Many people think this is them. You are correct and incorrect. If you know yourself and your life very well, then, it is. If you don't, then, you will need to discover this first. Now, where a business mentor comes in is their experience with situations similar to yours. They can help ensure that your business and wealth are growing in the right direction. They can help you prevent common mistakes rather than doing them. They can help guide you in all the steps in this framework. They can help you direct your time in creating value rather than making mistakes.

Even if you learn from a mistake, you can never take back the time you wasted on them. You can make mistakes, but only those that no-one could teach you to avoid.

Management

In medicine, we speak about management of patients. This is more than just giving painkillers to someone who hurt their thumb. This is understanding the patient as a person, a part of a family, community and society (including the economic workforce). It goes beyond taking care of what the body needs and encompasses a wider range of the facets that we, as people, are composed of, including the psychological aspects of disease, the social aspects of seeking medical care, and the financial implications of being sick. In the same way one should manage themselves – not isolating any part at the expense of the rest, but knowing how the parts interact to bring about success in your life. How to manage yourself:

1. Start with Why.

The way to manage a patient in medicine is straightforward, when you remove all the technical jargon. It begins with understanding 'why' a patient is seeing you or needs your help. So, seeing as you are the patient in this situation, ask yourself why you require help to change your life from one of struggle and poverty to an amazing life of success and contentment. In medicinal health, we call this seeking behavior, and the reason for that is most patients seek your help as a doctor. This is preferable, unless someone is in no condition to seek help, due to an accident or other emergency. Some people live their lives in a constant financial emergency, whether of their own doing or not. Unlike an unconscious patient, you should understand why you want financial success.

This is a difficult question to unravel, because most of us are conditioned to seek financial comfort (or discomfort) by our families, communities, and society, wherever we may be. We are taught to live for our lifetimes and make sure we can get by. This takes the excitement out of our potential-filled lives. In view of this, know why you think it's important to take your life where you want it to go; predict the future, and manage yourself.

Consider scenario 3 above, and ask yourself who the most experienced person to resuscitate your business and wealth is? I will give you a clue by mentioning three people it isn't:

1. Your girlfriend/wife.
2. Your mother.
3. This book and its author.

Does this help you? Quickly go to the mirror look at it face-on. Identify the person in looking at you, blinking at the same time you do. This is the person who is the most experienced about your life.

Remember that all other people who are in your life are there to give assistance and guidance. Welcome it, and don't avoid it. Use it to propel yourself to your best self, you best life, and your best wealth.

2. Follow with When.

The next important thing is to think of when you plan to change your life. Brian Tracy speaks of wealthy people as those who have decided to become wealthy and the poor as those who have not. Have you decided to become wealthy? Do you know when you would like to be wealthy? If you have made this decision and realize its seriousness, then, you will follow on to the next phase of the process of managing yourself. How, which people always want to start with, follows these two steps.

In the resus model, the timekeeper is the great equalizer. He just records what happens and shows it to you. Only you can decide what to do with your business as time passes. However, your decisions need to be time-based. This is what gives them significance. Like putting your hand on a hot stove, removing it is the appropriate action. Removing it quickly is the most beneficial action to you.

Who is Successful

One of the things people focus on when looking for opportunities is being at the right place at the right time. Equally important, however, is being the right you! Without this crucial participant, even the best places and the best of times may not be utilized to the extent that they should be. In view of this, one should be at the top of their game mentally, emotionally, and physically, in order to be most effective. Any situation or opportunity will only succeed as much as you allow it to succeed. If you play a small game, then, the situation will succeed in a small way – always be playing the bigger Game, and not putting limits on how much bigger it gets. Everything follows this formula in life:

Decision + Action = Results

This is true, no matter what you do, and will inevitably affect you, no matter what you do. The only difference is that some people's results are desirable to them, and others aren't. Let's take an example of you making a decision to become wealthy, but, then, not taking sufficient action. The result will be that you don't get wealthy. Remember: inaction is also an action and produces certain results.

Now, say you read and understand this book and apply it to your life. You decide you want to become wealthy. Take the appropriate action. The result will always lead to your wealth.

People with even more desire to change their lives will often change the formula to look like this:

Decision + *Massive* Action = *Massive* Results

The reason for this working in this way is because, as we mentioned before, taking the appropriate action will always lead to a certain result. This is a universal law.

So, if appropriate action A produces result B, it stands to reason that appropriate action 10A produces result 10B. The amazing thing about life is that the result may even be more than the perceived action and may be exponential in its growth and produce 100B. The challenge or opportunity here is that people often make decisions to take less than adequate action and hope for the best results. This is a mindset that needs to change if you are to achieve your goals.

Hope is a fix

I will share a little on my understanding of hope. It is a dangerous drug. In isiZulu we would call it isidakamizwa which loosely translatesto 'numbing the senses'. In your journey to wealth, hope is one of the many distractions that will play with your mind.

Hope gives the impression that you don't need to follow the laws of wealth creation, the laws of nature, and the laws of life. It makes talented people give half efforts and hope for the best. It convinces people that as long as they have enough of it, they can wait for someone else to do something.

It deceives the young, disempowers the middle-aged, and debilitates the old. Hope is a drug. Remember that before hoping that anything will happen. Hopium, as you should now remember, does not aid action; it delays it. In large enough quantities, it even causes inaction.

Don't do hopium!
– Odwa Gulwa

Here is an example you have heard before. How many years will it take you to start a successful business if you only hope to one day do it? Five, ten, twenty?

The answer is a resounding NEVER!!!

Do you choose to get a fix of hopium or get up and fix your life? I hope you choose the latter (like all dangerous medicines, doctors are allowed to prescribe them in small quantities).

Hopeless goals

Now that your goals have no hop(e)ium, you should fill the gap with action. The time available to change your situation may be limited. If someone collapses at home and, then, arrives in the emergency room unresponsive, as a doctor, your decision is clear – save a life. Your action must be appropriate and rapid to get closer to getting to the desired result ,which is a person being alive and well again.

Even a lay person will know from the entertainment shows that there is an urgency in saving someone's life and will even call out the health personnel if they seem to be dragging their feet. (I say call out, however, you know what I mean)

In your life, then – why is it that you decide that it's not worth the urgency? Why is it that you take other peoples' dreams more seriously than yours? If you don't stand up and take charge of your life and direct it where you want it to end up, who will? Well, decide today, and be unreasonable with its achievement.

Check the pulse of your wealth, and take appropriate action from today.

Remember, you cannot hope to make a decision and automatically have a result without taking action. This is known as fantasy, and you don't want this type of life, which exists in your own head. Take your wishes and dreams and turn them into reality. This is your ultimate goal in this life.

If you do not make wealth creation your number one priority, poverty will be your number one reality. Remember: wealth is abundance in all areas of your life. Wherever there is no abundance, the focus becomes lack.

Wealth can be likened to a healthy body. Like a well-rounded athlete, it is more than a warmth, pulse, and breathing. It is a ruddy, fit, toned body, able to withstand all forms of reasonable exercise thrown at it.

This may not sound right to you—it isn't meant to—it is what is happening to you right now. Look at the areas where you are not satisfied right now, are you not focusing on what is not there more than on what you are happy with? Is that not a reality of poverty created by you? Well you can now choose to create a focus on abundance. Once you do, you will attract more of it. Start attracting, talking about, and being grateful for all that you are happy with from today.

"Passionately pursue what you were purposed to do."
— Odwa Gulwa

Up Next

Thoughts and decisions represent the universal currency of your mind. Where you spend this currency determines where you are and where you are going. You need to learn how to create this currency, and how and where to spend it appropriately. You can almost never get a refund, but unspent, they eventually buy you regrets.

CHAPTER 5
DECISIONS, DECISIONS

The day you make the decision to become wealthy, a feaful cold may overcome you as you realize you don't know how to be wealthy. You may have heard it is difficult; you may even have avoided it at all costs. You may have heard people say things like, "It's lonely at the top." or, "Money can't buy you love, happiness, or even [insert desirable human virtue here]." The day I made the sure decision that I wanted to and would be wealthy, this same fear set in. My mind went into protection mode, as usual, to protect me from the possible pain associated with seeking and creating wealth.

Mind Your Mind

Your mind is a mechanism for survival and protection, not for wealth creation or helping you succeed. Know this and teach your brain to create the circumstances necessary for wealth creation. The time may come for the physical wealth to be questioned and sought by those whose job it is to count beans; they, too, will agree that, indeed, I am wealthy.

The brain is programmed to seek pleasure and avoid and protect you from pain. Once you understand what your brain is trying to do, teach it a new way to protect you. I consider not being wealthy a possibly painful experience. More importantly, being wealthy is a wonderful state of abundance, which I can enjoy and share with others. It is a dream I have had for a long time, and the impact I can make in this universe without wealth would be limited. I consider myself wealthy now, at this very moment, within the walls of this four-roomed abode in the somewhat dusty streets of Katlehong. I consider myself this way, because I certainly can. I do not look at my present circumstances to determine whether I am wealthy or not. I look within myself as a visionary of wealth and a pioneer of my wealth journey. I accept these things about myself daily through affirmations.

In his book, It Starts with Why, Simon Sinek explains that your reason why should always be the first point of call. With this clear in your mind, you can make focused and persistent strides toward your wealth, no matter how long it takes. When your why is strong enough, it is not a matter of if; it's a matter of when. Put differently, those who create wealth with why and when will always find a how.

How Deep Is Your Love?

As a part-time jogger I have tried many songs to motivate me along the route, from fast to slow, classic to dance music. There is, however, one song I can put on repeat and run my whole route: "How Deep Is Your Love?", by the Bee Gees. I resonate with this song, because it asks a perfect question for all journeys and destinations. It also asks a better question than simply, "Do You Love?"

I will ask you now to explore with me why you desire to be wealthy.

Why do you deserve abundance?

Why will humanity benefit from your wealth? Why wealth now, and not before?

Why wealth now, and not later?

Why do you want to reveal the wealthy you?

Remember it's your wealth, it's within you and all around you. You choose when you want access to it by the way you think. Therefore, wealth is a mindset, not just a fleeting thought. It is a practice, not a theory. Wealth is taught to you, and is as unnatural as breathing for a newborn baby, but it is as essential to life on the outside world for the human.

A fish out of water

Imagine a fish which uses its gills to extract oxygen from water suddenly being brought up to the land and being expected to breathe. You might say this sound unfair or cruel. The reality is that in the world today millions of babies are expected to do this daily. And no, babies don't have gills but 'breathe' in 'water' in their mother's womb.

Having lived an average of 36 weeks in a water filled cavity using a special symbiotic mechanism to extract oxygen from a red fluid called blood and living an "underwater existence" all babies are expected to come out and just breathe. The people who expect this of babies do so because they too went through the same process. Regardless of that many babies have tried to complain regarding this expectation. However due to their underdeveloped communication skills there are only heard as screaming beings from another world. By the time they can communicate, they have been taught to love their captors. Most of whose hearts they have captured.

Even more important than the above is that wealth is a decision, one only you can make. It's a journey you need to walk on your own, even in the midst of company, in the same way that no one can live your life for you. There are those who have defined wealth in a certain populist way to meet their ends and make it inaccessible to the minds of the many. Ignore these ones, too. They want you to believe that you can only be wealthy if you meet up to their measure of wealth. All too often, once you reach this imposed wealth, you may feel poorer still. Make your mind wealthy by finding out what your wealth is and, then, accumulating it in large amounts for yourself, your loved ones, your community, your nation, and the world.

> *Some people are so poor, all they have is money.*
> *— Bob Marley*

Remember, only you can create your unique wealth, so stop wasting time creating another people's wealth and pretending you find fulfillment from that. It's not that I am saying you are an island doing your own thing and caring about no-one else. I am saying that even two clerks at the same counter in a company earning the same minimum wage could be worlds apart in terms of wealth.

One could be whiling away time, hoping that one day, he would reach the top rung of the proverbial corporate ladder, meanwhile being used to further the dreams of the person who is at the top. The other could have realized his true wealth and be using the income from the same job to further his studies, so that he can become the musician he dreamed of being. While on the surface the two may seem alike, in reality, they are completely different.

Clock-In Mind

Philasande Libanzi, author and speaker, talks about the clock-in mentality amongst employees—the mind-boggling phenomenon where people are productive between the hours of eight in the morning and five in the afternoon. It is as though some mind control has been applied as a blanket over these people, and their patterns can be predicted literally like clockwork. It is the few who don't follow this pattern who allow their full potential to be explored voluntarily at any time of the day. These people are called different names like entrepreneurs, change-leaders, pioneers, visionaries, and square pegs. It's not that the 'round pegs' have no ideas or creativity—most of them actually do—it's that their ideas remain ideas forever. They live in Hopeville, a fictitious city in this book, which happens to be the biggest grower and exporter of *hopium.*

Super Wealth

Why do you want to be wealthy? What is it about you that will allow you to be wealthy? Let me ask it this way: will you allow the wealthy you to come out? Wealth is the superhero within you. Like Superman, you need a booth to transform from Clark Kent and into the real you. That is the purpose of Stop Working, Get Wealthy. It is a booth that is meant to reveal the true, wealthy you. Author and wealth coach Andrew Barsa puts it well in his book, The Millionaire Within.

The concept is that all you need to be a millionaire is already within you, and all you need to do is allow it to happen. Give the millionaire in you a chance to emerge and do what they were born to do. That millionaire is not just a mindless person with a million one-dollar bills. This person has mastered wealth in all areas where wealth can be created and decides which one is most prominent at any given time. If you think money can make you wealthy, you are right, and you are wrong. Like knowledge, money is not power in and of itself. The application and usage thereof suddenly makes it power.

> *With great power comes great responsibility.*
> – Uncle Ben

Like anything in life, we are taught how to be wealthy or how not to be wealthy. T. Harv Eker has already established this when he speaks of the money-blueprint. He teaches that regarding your financial wealth, it seems that there is a mental glass ceiling that controls whether or not you will ever be financially free. It is like a room with a thermostat that keeps the temperature in the room constant. This goes back even further than your thoughts, into your upbringing and your self-concept, and keeps you at a wealth level that your mind thinks will be most comfortable. Comfortable? For who? Your brain, which protects you from discomfort.

Your Entourage

Therefore, learn how to be wealthy. Then, apply the knowledge you learn about creating that wealth. There is no doubt that whatever wealth you desire in the world, someone is already an expert on it many times over. It is, therefore, paramount that you discover within yourself what wealth you desire and start learning how to create it.

Perhaps you desire relationship wealth. There are already thousands of people who have mastered the art of meaningful relationships. Find a few who match your values and learn from them. This is the way nature works. Of course, once you have learned from these people, you can always expand on these areas and add more and more. Whatever the case may be, start now. You can learn something valuable from anyone you meet in your journey. Don't discount those people. Apply their advice as appropriate to your values. Even Superman can learn from a young boy.

> *Surround yourself with people who reflect who you want to be and how you want to feel. Energies are contagious.*
> – Rachel Wolchin

You should always be associated with people of one accord with you. Let's assume since you are reading this book that you are seeking to discover your wealth. You need to associate yourself with people who have already discovered their wealth and people who are on the path to discovering their wealth. This will assist greatly in the maintenance of your goals in the same way birds of a feather flock together.

The journey, however, is still your own. Do not make your wealth interdependent on others. You will succeed, regardless of who agrees with your decision and helps you or hinders you along the way. No one can prevent you from becoming wealthy, not in a million years. Consider it this way – if someone tries to hinder your progress, it is like a body-builder, taking on more weight during his practice. After you overcome such hindrance, you will have one extra skill, that of overcoming such hindrances. What will happen if someone tries to hinder you in a similar way? They will find you invincible!

Perhaps, then, your situation changes, and you are no longer on the path to wealth that you imagined. Once you achieve wealth, you will have a more interesting story to tell and be stronger for it. Whatever the case may be, how you react to the situations you face will determine how they affect you mentally. Do your circumstances hold you back, or do they push your forward? The answer to such questions lies in your reaction to them. In the same way the people on your path are also either helping you forward or pulling you back, how they do it largely depends on your perspective and how you choose to react to them.

The Reporter

One day, a famous reporter was on his way to an interview. Along the way, when he was about to arrive at his destination, he met a beggar. The man asked for any change the reporter could spare. Seeing the beggar and feeling sorry for his situation, he gave him some change. The reporter realized he was early and was less than a block away from his destination.

He asked the beggar, "Why has your life turned out like this?" The beggar, grateful for the donation, looked up and mustered a reluctant grin. His face was wrinkled and weathered by his circumstances. "Well," he said, "I grew up in a broken home, my mother was poor, and my father was an abusive drunk." His face saddened further as he continued, "The area I grew up in was full of crime, gangs, and drugs. There was no one to look up to. What choice did I have, but to end up like this?"

The reporter listened intently and felt sympathy for the beggar. It was almost time for his interview, so he bid farewell to the beggar and said sincerely, " I hope it gets better."

He arrived at his interview of a successful business owner and investor who had come from nothing. A true rags-to-riches story. After discussing the details of the businessman's success, he had one closing question, "Why has your life turned out like this?" The man, with a twinkle in his eye, looked up and smiled. He was matured, but youthful in appearance. "Well," he said, "I grew up in a broken home, my mother was poor, and my father was an abusive drunk." His face brightened further as he continued, "The area I grew up in was full of crime, gangs, and drugs. There was no one to look up to. What choice did I have, but to end up like this?"

The beggar and the businessman were brothers, raised in the same home.

You Already Have It

There is nothing more powerful in the wealth journey than believing actively that you have that wealth already. You may ask how you can believe this.

> *Therefore, I tell you, whatever you ask for in prayer, believe that you have received it, and it will be yours.*
> *– Mark 11:24, The Bible*

Regardless of your religious affiliations or disaffiliations, the above verse describes the true power of the mind. The mind is divided into two main parts, namely the conscious mind and the subconscious mind. The conscious mind interacts with the world on a more direct level during the waking hours and is responsible for the day-to-day functioning of a person. It utilizes your senses to create meaning of the world around it.

The subconscious mind, on the other hand, is a massive library of information, containing all the information you have ever experienced in your life. It is the job of the conscious mind to determine which of this information is needed and retrieved at any particular time.

The World Is Yours

Why did I tell you this fun fact? Well, because understanding your own mind is, perhaps, the most important thing you will do toward understanding yourself. Within your mind, therefore, is a world created by your interaction with your environment and the people in your life. This 'artificial' world is your reality, and based on this mental reality, your outer world will be created. The physical reality is based on the workings of your mental reality. Understand this very well, and use it to your advantage.

When you apply this knowledge correctly, you will start to realize that, in fact, you are in control of whether you become wealthy or not. It is no one's responsibility to make you wealthy, and, indeed, even if you are showered with money, this does not make you wealthy. No one can study a degree on your behalf and, then, transfer it to you – at least not currently. In the same way, no one can create wealth and, then, transfer it to you. You need to do that on your own, and, then, you will find that money and other signs of wealth will follow. Wealth is the mentality you need to control large amounts of money and resources and make them work for you.

Personality Wealth

The question of passion always arises when it comes to wealth. I solve it in three ways. Firstly, by questioning what passion is: dictionary.reference.com defines passion as, "Any powerful or compelling emotion or feeling, as love or hate." This word is, apparently, derived from the word for suffering, as experienced by Christ on the cross. Effectively, this means the willingness to pay the price for what you love. Many people love many careers and only wish or hope they could do them. Few are willing to pay the price. They want to achieve their dreams, without ever waking up to make them happen. Remember Hopeville?

Well, you may be wondering if your passion can bring about your wealth. It can. This is the ideal where everyone should be. It involves finding your values first, your why, then, aligning your goals with these and taking action to produce the required results. The starting point here is to find your values, as they will give light to your passions and, once you align your goals to these, you will start to experience more fulfillment from what you do.

Passion Chart

Look at fig 5.1, the passion chart.

Smallest Circle

The smallest circle indicates the location where all these things happen. It's either in the inner world or the outer world. You have limited influence on where things happen, but if you understand, you can influence changes in the correct world. To recap, inner world is thoughts, feelings, knowledge, and spirit. Outer world is composed of actions and results.

Medium Circle

Begin with your values, which define your why. Finding these means exploring your passions, finding them, and defining your journey.

Goals are next and should align with your values. If you neglect this alignment, your goals will be unattainable, as they will expend more energy than you have. A good example of this is when people seek financial wealth without aligning the means of attaining it with their values. This is when burnout occurs, because each subsequent step in the cycle expends energy you cannot renew. If the inner world is aligned, it gives intense energy to the outer world, and vice versa.

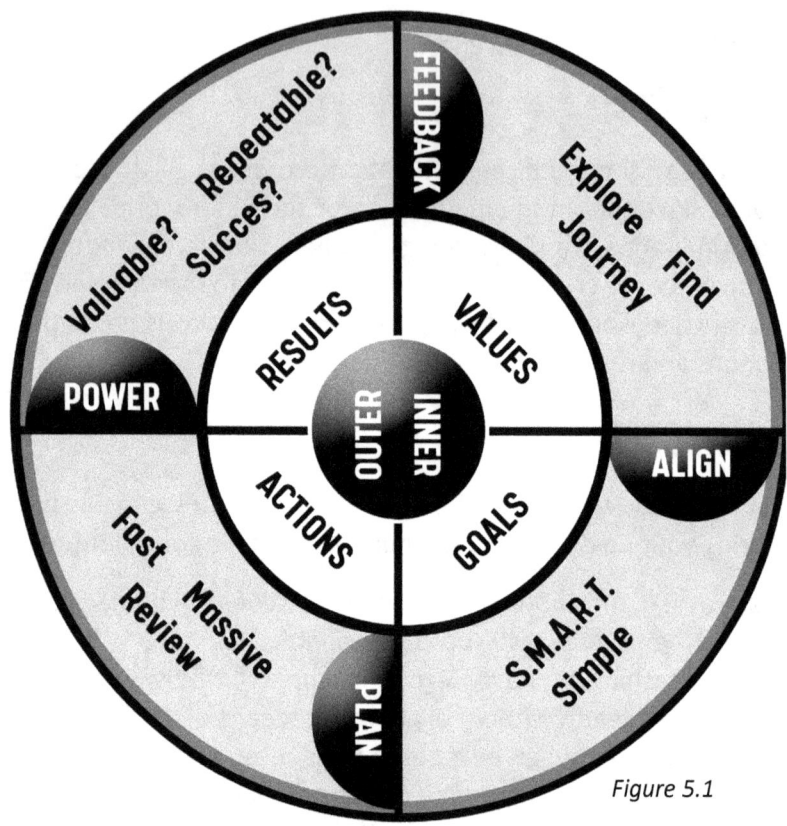

Figure 5.1

Your goals, then, are based on the S.M.A.R.T acronym by George Doran. They should be simple in their wording and should leave no loopholes as to interpretation. Using these goals, you should plan actions that make success enjoyable. If your goals are S.M.A.R.T., then, your actions will be deliberate. If not, you will waste a lot of energy. Review the actions you take against the goals and the results. If the results are what you find desirable, repeatable, and valuable, then, continue your actions. If not, reassess your values and your goals, then, change the actions where necessary, until the result is as you desired.

Once the results are desirable, repeatable and valuable, you can change your actions by making them more massive than before. You can also reduce the time between certain groups of actions. Consider the formula below:

Decision + Action = Results

Tough Decisions

The decision is probably the most difficult part of this whole equation. Why? Because most people don't know that it is made up of values and goals that are aligned. They often cannot make a decision, because they don't find their values and almost always imitate other people's goals. In the times we live in, people are making less and less decisions for their own future. More commonly, decisions are outsourced to other people, technology, and the Internet. When people are coughing, they will go onto Google.com™ and type in, "Why am I coughing?" The answers will usually make them decide to see a doctor. This is not a criticism toward this method, but definitely one of the easiest ways to get yourself worked up about a cough.

The point is that decisions should not be outsourced; one should collect all the necessary advice from the most suitable advisors. Reading is a form of advice, if you look at the origin of the word. Gather all of it, and use the available facts to make the decision. Remember when it's your decision, you cannot blame anyone. This, too, may be a reason for this outsourcing of decisions – finding a scapegoat. You are responsible for your own life, and no one can be blamed for how it turned out. Indeed, certain people may have done different things to you, but the final decision on how those things affected you rests on you.

In the arena of wealth creation, I learned very quickly that making a decision is paramount to success. Do not, of course, rush into things without a clue on what the possible outcomes and risks might be. Do, however, practice learning about the facts of the situation; seek proper advice, and, then, use it in the most efficient way to make your decision. No good opportunity is going to be lying around waiting for you to hope it into existence. Opportunities are few and far between in *Hopeville*, but can be found in abundance in Actionton, a neighboring city, where action comes by the ton.

To strengthen this point, let's consider the following situation. You are a front passenger in a car. The driver is your child, who recently got their license. You reach an intersection where the traffic light turns yellow. Your child then speeds up a little, as if to cross the intersection, but slams on the brakes, bringing the car to a stop, smack bang in the middle of the intersection. You, fortunately, are a good parent, and you don't scream or make them feel stupid and irresponsible. You calmly switch on the hazard lights as you apologize to the other motorist and request they wait as you cross to the other side. Apart from all the advice you will give to your child, much of which they will take with them for the rest of their lives, you say this, "Make a decision, my child."

To you I say, "Make a decision, my reader."

A Fork In The Road

When making decisions without aligned values and goals, it is like being in an enormous maze. A place where you do not know up from down. Each choice before you presents numerous possibilities, which can paralyze the uninitiated. This is your initiation.

Consider two people at a fork in the road. One is undecided and waits at the fork looking left and, then, right. The other decides to take the path on the left and runs down as fast as she can. When she gets to the end of the path, she realizes that it's not where she wants to be. She quickly turns back and runs toward the fork in the road, only to meet up with the undecided person. She whizzes past her and, now, takes the other path in the fork. While running, she thinks she hears the other person ask, "What's back there? Should I follow you?" She pays no attention to her and, instead, continues on her path, enjoying the scenery on the path she now knows is the path for her. The other person goes back to the fork in the road and wonders frantically what could have been so horrible about the path on the left that she came back running. She feels her decision has been made for her.

Whatever scary thing the other person saw or experienced, she is not going to wait around to see what it is. Her decision to do nothing is her decision, and whatever consequences she finds herself in as a result will be solely upon her. This issue will come up again, dear reader, so decide now that you are a great decision-maker in every way.

New Innovation Is Collaboration

When I look at the traditional business world as I see it, there is a lot of selfishness within it. I am not pointing fingers, because I am included within it. The traditional way of doing things is that I will get what I want, use it, and, then, if there is anything left over, I may consider helping the next person.

> *Collaboration is the new innovation.*
> *– Octavius Phukubye*

Firstly, I believe that everyone, no matter who they are have something positive to offer to the world. Not everyone chooses to offer this, though. Secondly, people live in a world of scarcity, as mentioned in a prior chapter. A world in which there is not enough of anything, and one should get what he needs to at whatever cost.

True Wealth

True wealth begins with a true you. A real you that is one with your values and goals and, therefore, passion. True wealth uses that passion to serve others and de-serves a fair exchange of value in what means the most to them. As said earlier, the further you are from your values and passions, the more skewed your view of wealth is.

More specifically in the realm of wealth creation, people assume that riches are scarce. Because of that, they put others down in order to get ahead. This type of thinking may work for a short while, but it will never create true wealth. The little wealth it might create will not be sustainable and will not be duplicable or transferrable. Always make sure that you are true to the virtues you believe in. That way, you are setting yourself up to find true contentment and fulfilment in wealth.

Take, for example, a business built on bribery, without deciding whether it is morally right or wrong. It cannot be sustained, simply because the successors of the business may not be willing to continue the bribery culture. The other reason may be that the person to be bribed no longer accepts bribes. Whatever you eventually decide to do, remember that you are building a legacy, not a get-rich-quick scheme, and your business should reflect that. In the end, there is no business—only you and a reflection of you in the mirror called business.

Everything is in The Booth

The point I was trying to get to is regarding a new way of thinking, one to be used by the wealthy and those who are creating wealth. The world is abundant with everything you need. The world is filled with the resources, people and opportunities you need. The finding and attracting them to you is the challenging part. It is either difficult or easy. Whatever you decide will be your truth. If you were raised to understand wealth to be difficult and unattainable, it will be as such, unless you actively and deliberately change your mindset.

A simple change in the words you use to this about wealth is a great start:

Creating my wealth may be challenging in the beginning, but has become easier and easier. Challenge is a word with a better energy about it, and don't you want to be someone who overcame challenges?

Make sure you find affirmations aligned to your values that empower you. Use them daily to transform your inner world. Think of Superman in the booth before he comes out. What do you think he thinks and says to himself?

"I hope I will be able to do this."

"Last time it was difficult. Now, it's going to be impossible."
"Maybe I shouldn't come out. Can't Batman solve this?"

"It's not my JOB to save people all the time."

"These people aren't paying me, should I risk my life for them?"

Probably none of the above, since he is a fictional character. For humans, though, if any of these thoughts do manage to creep in you need to have a counter-measure to dispel them. When you come out of the booth, you need all your focus on winning the challenge that has arisen. Affirmations are like anti-kryptonite. You are not wishing kryptonite away; you are prepared to overcome it.

What is the booth? Each thought, minute, hour, day, and lifetime.

Too Much Wealth, Too Few People

The world is abundant, and there is no shortage of wealth of any kind. Ther is, however, a shortage of people willing to pay the price for their wealth, and this is what needs to change. Why do I say there is a shortage? Many people are in jobs that make them unhappy, living lives of people they don't know and spending money they don't have. Hardly anyone is in a purposeful job that fulfills them, solving real world problems and getting paid what they consider to be fair and using their finances in a responsible way. I am no exception and that is the reason for this book. It is not for me to look down from the comfort of my high horse and sneer at the "commoners"; it is to change the status quo and begin living a life of significance.

Who, then, decides that our lives are significant? It is the individual, himself, who decides. Make sure you live a life of significance now, and don't wait until you have more money or more time, because it will likely not happen. Become the person you desire to be in the future right now, and do the 'things' that person does. As time goes on, you will have the things that person has. It sounds too simple, doesn't it? If you always wante right now, and do thed to give ten percent of your income to church or charity, begin now, while earning $1,000 per month, because it's not going to be easier when you're earning $100,000 per month. The person who couldn't afford to give $100 to charity will definitely not give $10,000 not because it is impossible, but only because it is difficul -okay,challenging, smarty pants.

Overcome this challenge while your income is challenged. You will then be a much better overcomer when your income over comes. Is that not a good challenge to have in your life? Decide today that you will always have an overcoming income.

Up Next

Be grateful for where you are now. Picture the place you are now as a stop over for the rest of your journey. Enjoy its beauty, without being distracted from the end goal. Learn from its challenging nature, without being defeated into inaction. If you are not grateful, you may not realize that it's a portal to the next journey.

CHAPTER 6
THE SALES LIFE YOU ARE ALWAYS SELLING

From before you were born, you were selling. This is why, even now, you are still selling. Selling, I believe is what humans were made for, and I will explain why I think so. Selling is simply communication, which is expressed slightly differently than other communication. The only difference is how people choose to apply it, and the fact that they keep trying to separate the two from one another. I view them as the same thing, and because of this – as Barry Mitchell teaches – I apply this in everyday life. In other words, all communication can be viewed as selling, and only our attitude to selling would make this difficult to imagine. Take some time to think about this.

People are always buying

Of course, if we are always selling, then, we are also always buying, and this completes the selling cycle. The only thing that makes the difference is what we are buying. We sell and buy from ourselves from the time we are conceived, and we continue to buy and sell alone and to other people. This may sound highly philosophical, but bear with me as I break things down. All thoughts in mind right now are examples of ideas you bought or bought into. Even the expression "buying into" something suggests that buying is a mental process. The ideas you express to others and the desires and dreams you have are examples of things you are selling to others and to yourself.

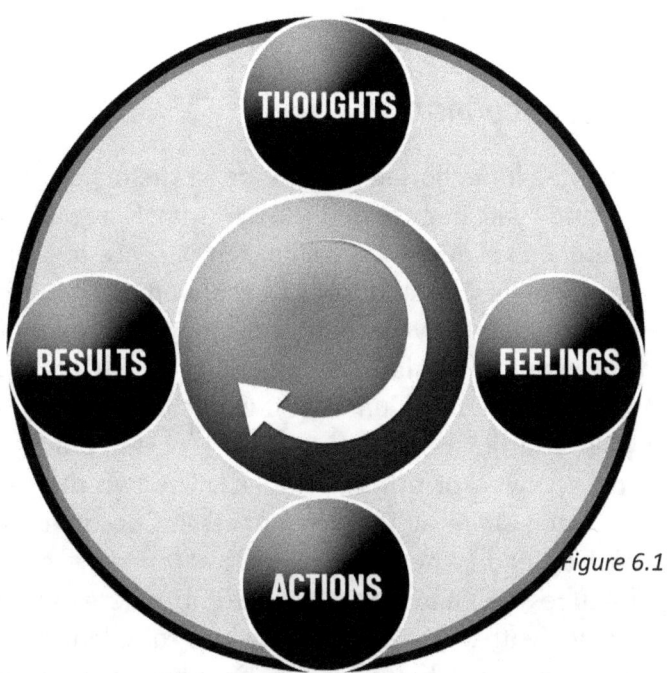

figure 6.1

We share common origins

If you remember the chart from chapter 2 (6.1), it shows that thoughts are first in the process of manifestation. So, where do our thoughts come from? They were created by our environment and our conditioning, as a result of what we were exposed to the most

in our early years. They were formed and accepted as reality in our middle years. In our later years, we practice them as the truth and even teach them to others. The saddest of these is conditioning the future generations to have the same limiting thoughts as the previous generation had. Is there a solution to this? I think it starts with you – be aware what you sell to yourself, because, most likely, you will sell it to your children. It is neither right, nor wrong. The only question is whether you want your children to have the same thoughts.

Biology of conception

I could give you a long, boring description of the biology of human conception, and I will, but not in this book. Mainly because you can Google™ good videos about it. I will make reference to it, however, as it applies to sales. The man sells to the woman that they need to share their love and have a child, and the woman buys in (in the paternalistic, idealized world). The fastest and most focused sperm then sells to the available ovum that it wants to fertilize it, and the ovum buys in, shutting out all other sperm (or else buying in bulk, which results in twins or other multiples). The two then sell each other to fuse and share all that they have and become one. They then sell each other on why they should move from where they meet (usually the tubes) to a new home – the womb, where they will have space to grow. If either one doesn't buy into this idea, it results in an ectopic pregnancy. If, however they both buy in and move, they then put their roots down in a prime spot in the womb and begin to multiply at great speeds. The selling here is a frenzy. Some get a better deal than others, getting to be brain cells. Others don't get so great a deal and get the other end of the body, better known as the anus. I could go on, but this journey never ends, until your body sells your mind on a reason to separate, resulting in death.

DNA joint venture

One of the most important steps in the above description is the sharing of the DNA, the blueprint by which the body is developed. The units of these DNA-containing structures are called chromosomes, and most humans have 46 in total – 23 from the mother, and 23 from the father. This is an amazing clue about how life and business work, too. Remember, if it's good enough for the perpetuation of the human race for all these years – it's good enough for your business and for your life, too. There is an amazing power in collaboration, and for the most part, it is underutilized.

Internal exponential growth

If you ever wanted an analogy of how your business should grow, you would not have to look far. Just look to the growth of a human inside the womb and the subsequent growth after birth. If startups could grow like that, there would be a different world to live in. One of the biggest misconceptions is that businesses should grow slowly to last – this is not true. In the right conditions (the womb for the baby), with the correct funding and coaching (the umbilicus and the mother), and the correct legislative framework for small businesses (the amniotic fluid), all businesses can and will succeed. This may sound simplistic, but it isn't, and if you draw some of these analogies into your own business, you may realize you are trying to conceive a baby and grow it to term in the desert. It is not enough to have the sperm and ovum come together.

The origin of sales

Dr. John Demartini explains the origin of sales as coming from the exchange of energy and as a result the unification of spirit and matter. How he reaches this conclusion is remarkable and may confuse some (including this author). It is, however, something

I continue to think about as I walk my journey, and it starts to become more and more apparent that it is true in my life. Whether it is true in your life is a matter of perspective. It starts off with the understanding that we are all multifaceted beings with spiritual and physical sides. Others may refer to this as the mind and the body.

Divine sales events

Every day of our lives, divine sales events happen to us. One of them is waking up alive and selling the world and the universe a reason for our existence. Once awake, we can choose what to do with our thoughts and, therefore, our lives. Robin Banks points out that once awake, no one forces on you the thoughts that you will think for the day – you choose them. Be that as it may, we sometimes still choose thoughts that do not serve us. On the other hand, Brian Tracy says that our thoughts are so powerful as to change our destination when we change them. Sell to yourself the divine ability to change what people call your destiny, instead of just buying into your current situation or circumstances. You have the ability to choose another fate, one of your own creating. Take charge of your future right now. Peter Drucker says, "The only way to predict the future is to create it." What are you creating right now?

True sales involve your whole being

You may have all heard the line from The Boiler Room movie "A-B-C: always be closing." It speaks to the requirement of sales people to always be thinking about closing the sale – the sale of what? Whatever you sell. It is easily summarized as – begin with the end in mind. From the time you start thinking about selling anything, think of how to complete it successfully. Never go into a situation thinking you will fail, because you will surely be correct.

Practically, it means being mentally ready in the way you think about your success. It means speaking what you WANT and not what you

DON'T WANT. It means acting the way a person who has succeeded acts. Dressing like they dress. Feeling like they feel. Without this foundation, you will find it very difficult to succeed in what you want. Every fiber of your body should feel like the sale is closed – then, you will find, amazingly, that it is. Too many people doubt themselves and, then, go out, expecting others to believe in them. Sell it to yourself first. If you wouldn't buy you, why would the next person?

Always be selling

I will take it a step further and say, "Always be selling." This is not in contradiction with what I said in the beginning—that we are ALWAYS selling. The only difference is that you must stay aware of what you are selling – Always Be Selling. If you are doing it anyway, wouldn't you rather be selling what you want to sell – not what you are forced to sell by others, by your environment, or by circumstances? It may involve associating yourself with those already selling what you want to sell, modeling them, and, then, finding your unique product. This is metaphorical speak about your attitude, thoughts, words, and actions – SELL what you WANT to sell.

Helps keep focus

When you live the Sales Life, then, you determine your fate; you create your life. Focus on the things you want in your life, because you are aware of what you take in (your associations) and what you put out (your circle of influence), and as such, you will get the results that come from those actions. The Sales Life is a mentality—and a powerful one at that—if you focus on its implementation. The trick is the focus, and, unfortunately, it sometimes eludes us, but makes itself found again, as long as we seek it. Focus makes the difference between torch and laser. One can only illuminate, while the other can cut through gems. Focus cannot be overstated and remains the great equalizer. If you can focus, you can do anything. What are you not focusing on that you need to? Sell yourself the need to refocus today.

Determines tangible outcomes

All tangible outcomes that you desire begin with a simple thought. A thought that you nurture becomes tangible reality. Just because you don't know which thoughts you created and nurtured more than others doesn't mean you are not responsible for the outcomes they bring. The sooner you realize that you are responsible for everything that happens to you, the better, and you can control this to your advantage – or not control it, which may be to your detriment. Look at everything you have all around you. Think of all the things you have, good and bad – they are there because you created them through your thoughts. Accept this, even though it might be difficult to understand, and use that to determine where your life goes from here on.

Perhaps you have too many good things in your life – an unlikely way to think. More likely, you are thinking about all the things you don't like about your life and, as a result, are creating more of them. Take, for example, your JOB – whatever your thoughts about jobs, you are likely to be in a job of that nature. I am not speaking of the hopes you have about your future JOB somewhere on the greener side of the grass. I am speaking about the thoughts you have about your boss and colleagues right now. These are the thoughts that created the life you have now. The thoughts you think today will determine the life you live from this second forward.

Technical life skills

My mentor and coach, Barry Mitchell, taught me many lessons in sales, including how to be confident and direct. I am still working on most of the things he taught me, even in my life today. Amongst other achievements, he is the best sales and business coach in

Africa, having been taught by Blair Singer. Most of the lessons in this chapter are from his teachings, and I have just found ways to apply them to my life.

Find and keep customers

Peter Drucker says that the *purpose* of a business is to find and keep customers, while the goal of a business is to make a profit. In traditional business, thinking in this way will set most businesses apart from the rest in a big way. It requires leaders who will need to apply this first internally—with the employees being the customers. Then, it requires teaching the employees to do the same externally, with clients.

If one applies this to one's personal life, one can say the purpose of life is to find and keep relationships, with the goal being mutual growth. You can really replace this with your own meaning. For me, it is important to find and keep relationships and ensure that there is mutual growth in them, whatever it takes. I believe that was the original intention of Ubuntu, before it was hijacked by those who wanted it to remain an unattainable ideology. With this mindset, your personal relationships will be quite interesting and amazing, especially because you need to make them together.

Handling objections

In sales, objections are what people do and say to avoid buying from you. In life, these are the things that some call failing. What if they say NO?

What if they LAUGH at me? What if I look RIDICULOUS? What if they EMBARRASS me?

Those are just some examples of the things we say to ourselves to avoid getting objections in life and in sales. The fear of objections comes from our acquired fear of rejection. It is one of the biggestreasons why people don't think of themselves as being salespeople. Try as you might, objections and, sometimes, rejections will come. When you know and prepare for them, you will no longer see them as deterrents, but, rather, as opportunities. You will see feedback, rather than failure.

Ask questions

The greatest key to maintaining the sales life is asking questions, but not just any questions. Ask questions that leave the possibility for success. This applies when you are selling to yourself, as well as when you are selling to others.

Your mind is designed to answer questions—don't you think so? Just now, your mind gave you an answer to the previous question. A great goal is to make sure that the answers your mind gives are empowering ones. Do you think that will help you succeed?

If you still don't understand, let me explain it like this. Your mind is pre-occupied with thoughts – thousands at a time go

through your mind every second. These thoughts are answers to questions your mind is continually asking, sometimes consciously and, most times, unconsciously. An example is when you do something you are not proud of and, then, ask yourself: "What is wrong with me?" Your brain is designed to answer this question with whatever answer it would like – and yes, there will always be an answer. Mostly, we allow our brain to have free will regarding the answer. We should start off with a destination in mind. When you know the destination, you can find all the routes that can lead to it. I will show you another chart that we saw in chapter 5 (fig 6.2)

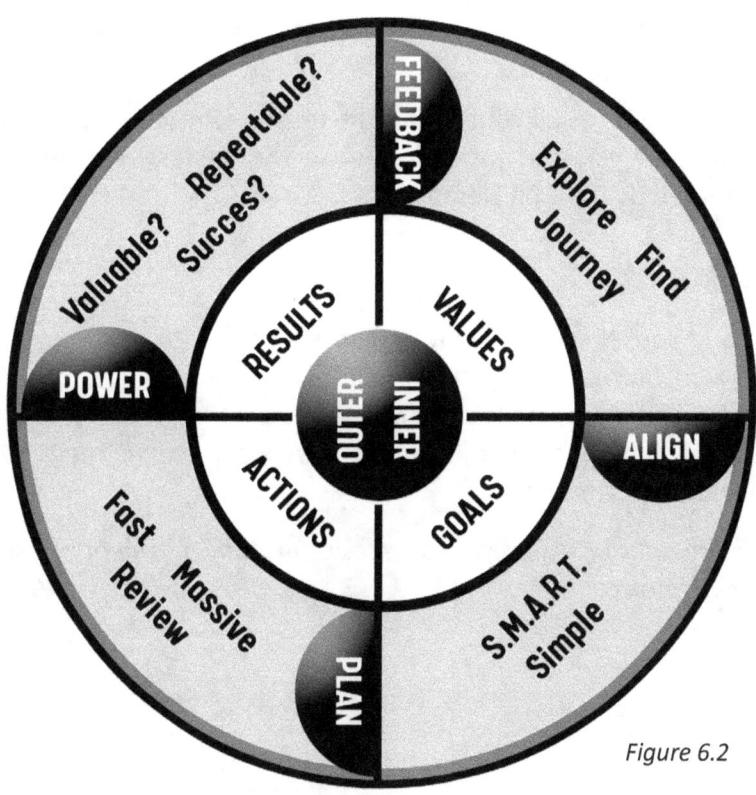

Figure 6.2

The sales start from the inner world with values. Once you have sold yourself to your values, you can sell yourself the correct goals for your life. Your actions thereafter will be determined against the values and goals. When you see the results from the prior three, you can sell yourself on modifying the actions, so you can produce results that are more in line with your values. This causes a reinforcement of the values and achievement of the goals, which causes more action and produces more of the desirable results. I could go on forever, but I won't. To explore the opposite effect: if your values and goals are not in agreement, your actions will be half-hearted, and your results will be confusing. This reinforces the mentality that you are not in control of the results in your life, that it doesn't help to have values or goals.

The first step is to sell yourself on the reason why you should know your deepest values. I periodically use the Values Determination Test created by Dr. John Demartini.

Up Next

We have spoken about many important things on our journey to wealth. In the next chapter, we will speak about the "Stop". The title of the book is 'Stop Working, Get Wealthy'. We will speak about what I mean by "stopping", because many people think they should turn in their resignation.

Don't fire your boss just yet. Let's look carefully at one of the stops you must make.

AN ATTITUDE OF GRATITUDE

CHAPTER 7

Depending on your 'transport' to wealth, you will need pitstops—filling stations, if you like. Gratitude can be likened to the fuel that powers your wealth vehicle. It is a principle that has been preached, but hardly practiced. Regardless of the vehicle, when the fuel is finished, there is no movement. Make sure to regularly fill up during the easy and difficult stages of the journey. In other words, it is the singular most significant quality of a wealthy person.

You will agree with me that wealth is relative; there are degrees of comparison for something like financial wealth. That is why you have world rankings on different resources, like *Forbes Magazine,* which ranks people around the world, according to the net worth of their financial wealth. The gratitude principle works in this way: you should be grateful for what you have, before you are given more. This is such a strong principle, because all wealth is an accumulation of smaller parts, and, therefore, all the parts are necessary for the whole to exist. If you don't appreciate the smaller parts, then, by implication, you don't appreciate the whole.

Here is an example: you want to be a millionaire, and that is your ultimate financial goal for this year. The one unlikely way that this could happen is that someone could give you one million dollars in one go, and that would be that. The other way is that you could collect one dollar from a million people for selling them something they find useful. If you are a person who doesn't appreciate one dollar and sees it as something not worth collecting, why would you get a million of those useless things? Therefore, appreciating the smaller parts that make up your whole is imperative. That useless dollar, if you have one million dollars, is the difference between you being a millionaire and a just another guy with a lot of dollars. It is that important, and it applies to all the areas of your wealth. Be grateful for the little things, because they make up the bigger things. Not only that, you should celebrate the smaller things, because now, you will celebrate a million and one times. Most of us are waiting for one final celebration.

Similarly, don't let your gratitude be taken away because of envy. Whatever you have, you may always find someone who has more of it. Be a person who races against yourself, not against other people. Be the best and most effective you that you can. In this way, you will have the best appreciation for who you are. Remember, no one is better than you or smarter than you, however, there are people who are closer to their purpose and true wealth than you are to yours. A key is to find your passion (see passion chart) and cultivate it, to give you the results you desire.

Wealth your way

I define wealthing as the process of discovering your journey to ultimate abundance. It has been used in other ways by many authors. For our purpose, this is what it means:

Wealthing is a way of life that is different from the mentality of exchanging time for money, of being productive only between 9 and 5, of doing just enough to prevent ourselves from being fired. Having said that, wealthy people must still work, so what makes them wealthy? It is the mentality with which they operate that makes them different. Not the things they accumulate. Our goal should be to accumulate the mindset that creates wealth, which no one can ever take away from you. Once you start, you will find that in all aspects of your life, wealthing will permeate.

Ultimate Wealth

I have always wondered if there is a universal wealth that everyone needs to be wealthing to. In the first chapter, we established that there are seven areas that we can create wealth within (fig 1.1), and anything you can think of can fit into these. The question remains, though, what unifies them all, if anything. Tony Robbins speculates that the end-point of everything is the feeling that all the accomplishments give us. The feelings of contentment, gratitude, or even love are among some of the feelings we all desire, and where all our efforts lead to. Others believe that the endpoint of it all is the spiritual fulfillment brought about by the way one's life was led. This is the endpoint of all religions and faith systems. The notion that the Greater Being will evaluate your temporary existence and decide which outcome is acceptable for your eternal existence.

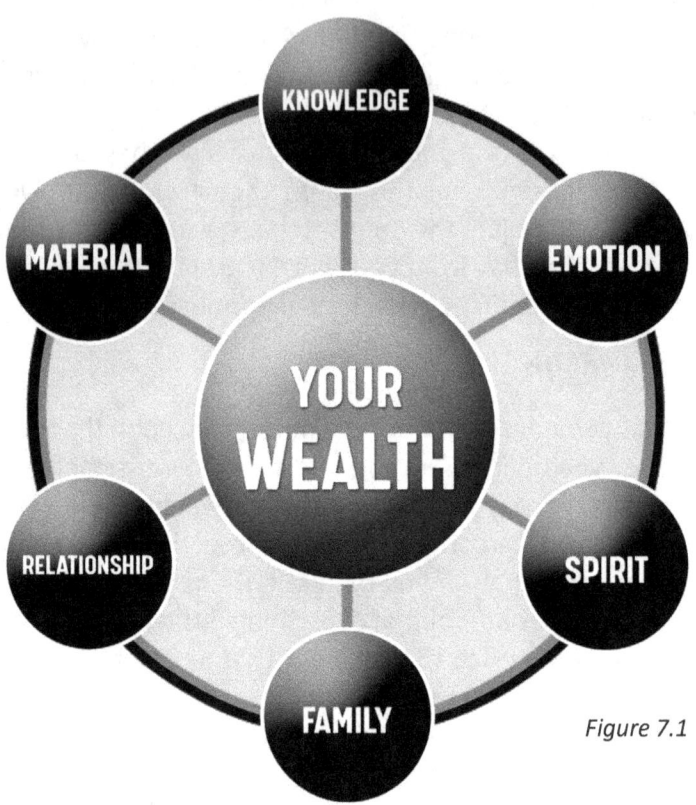

Figure 7.1

People only ask these questions when they reach wealth in its essence in a particular facet. So, it's not that they are unanswerable, but, rather that they are unasked. I am not saying I know the answers, but I would rather more people were asking the question – what is the universal wealth that all humans seek, and is it really universal? Where should we be wealthing to? Each time I arrive at an answer, it brings another question. Each time I arrive at a destination, it is the beginning of another journey.

Is this question really that important, though? I think it is, because you will one day want to know what the point of it all was. I find myself sometimes asking myself why I would even bother creating wealth

– is it not all meaningless, anyway, as King Solomon discovered? These and more questions keep me pondering at this life, but also motivate me to ask more pressing questions, like; what difference can I make in my life, in this world and in the universe? Will I be remembered at all? I ask these questions, because in my short life, I have already been present at the end of many people's lives. Certainly, more than the average man, because of my profession, and because of this, I always ask myself every day

– what happens to these people now? What of all their wealth? What of all their poverty? I am certain that this question will always plague humans until the end of the world.

One of the feelings I think should be present at the end of one's life is gratitude. I believe that gratitude is the ultimate attitude. One that wealthy people who create and sustain wealth always possess. This is the attitude I am always cultivating within myself. It is a wonderful feeling, and one with many levels. Let's explore three of these levels.

Gratitude is a Person

When gratitude is likened to a person, he is like the person who seems like he has nothing, but always tells you how blessed he is. We have seen such people: they never ask for anything from you and make you feel ungrateful, because you realize how lucky you are to be who you are and have what you have. This person approaches situations asking what he can do, not what can be done for him. Wherever Gratitude goes, his friend is always behind him. He goes by the name Humility.

Think in your life that whenever Gratitude leaves Humility too far behind, Vanity starts to seduce him. This analogy was confusing to me at first, but the more I thought about it, the more

it made sense. I find that my mind has a way of doing that to me. I realized that gratitude is a way of being, rather than an action or a noun. It describes a certain level of faith in the Greater Being or the Universe. It is the cosmic magnet to whatever you desire. This is not a theory I came up with, but, rather, an explanation for something I see happening regularly in everyday life.

Gratitude owns everything

Everything people acquire and keep for any significant period of time is directly proportional to the amount of gratitude they possess for those things. By extension, I figure that gratitude owns everything, for as long as you have gratitude and the thing, it will remain yours. If you lose gratitude, but keep the thing, it is likely that very soon, you will lose the thing, too. If, however, you lose the thing and keep the gratitude – in a short space, you will be able to acquire that thing again in a better form. Finally, if you have never had the thing, but build up gratitude for it – you are more likely to get it when you take the same action as someone who doesn't have the gratitude.

This is an immensely important principle to understand, as it separates the "rich" from the "wealthy". It allows money to have different abilities, depending on the unique individual possessing it. It is the reason why one shouldn't desire something, just because someone else has it.

Gratitude allows you to appreciate the things you have, so the Universe knows that you will appreciate the things you want. If you then desire or envy someone else's things, it is unlikely that you will appreciate them as they do, because you desire from the physical outer reality and have not, as yet, created the inner world equivalent of those things. Those things may, in the end, be burdensome to you, because you desired them without attaching the required gratitude.

Relating to the passion chart previously shown (fig 7.1), find your values first. Then, create the goals of the things you desire.

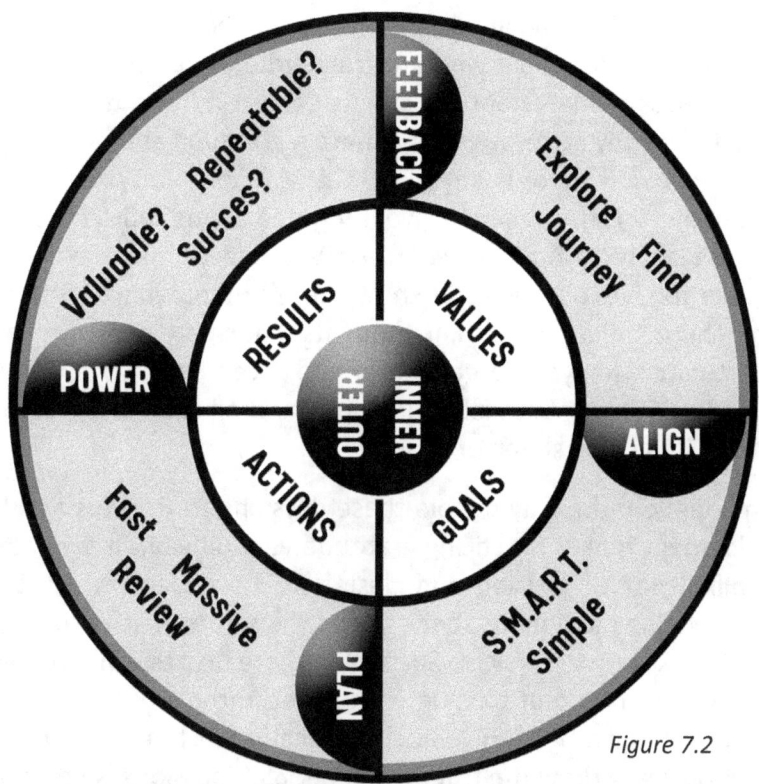

Figure 7.2

Gratitude, then, owns everything, meaning whatever you are not grateful for is likely to slowly disappear from your thoughts; you will speak less of it, and, finally, it will disappear from your life, whether literally or figuratively. Sadly, this not only happens with things, but also with people. Be grateful for the people in your life, too.

Gratitude Gives Freely

We have established that gratitude brings humility, and that as a result, one cannot be arrogantly grateful. However, where gratitude really excels is in its ability to bring about generosity. I will go as far as to say that all people who are truly grateful for what they have are generous givers. Gratitude begets generosity, and the converse is also true. Truly generous people have a gratitude about them that is unshakable. If there is anything that will make you truly grateful for your life, it is the ability to give freely and abundantly. It creates a situation in which you are in control of your life, so much so that you are able to give, because you know there's more where that came from. This enables you to think thoughts that create more and more opportunities for you to get more, and, eventually, you will have more. This is an unbreakable principle, and all the major religions espouse it in some shape or form.

In my opinion, the way people these days choose careers and find employment makes practicing gratitude very difficult. It is a matter of ability, not of passion and desire. You can become a doctor without being passionate about it, and the same abilities could just as well make you a physicist. Such jobs where no passion is required in the description, but passion is expected throughout your career in large amounts. Does the way the education system works around the world really draw the trueness of people's passions, so that they are doing the things that make them feel alive, or is it a conveyor belt, meant for the fulfilment of targets and quotas? Why, then, don't schools comprehensively teach us from a young age how to discover who we truly are, why we are here, and what we need to serve people with?

Be grateful and generous in all your dealings with yourself and others. Then, wealth will be your friend forever. Dr. Marko Saravanja says it perfectly: "Those who give unconditionally, will receive abundantly." Make this a practice in your everyday thoughts, and it will become a part of your life.

Up Next

What is the definition of wealth that you use? Does it have an influence on what work you choose to do? Now that you know about wealthing, are you able to identify the areas you want wealth in? If your job cannot answer your wealth questions, it is likely stopping you from becoming wealthy. Let's look at how I define it for myself, and you can start a framework of your own.

CHAPTER 8

WEALTHING IT
BODY WEALTH

I have spoken briefly about the types of wealth that exist. There are three types of basic wealth that supersede financial success. The first—and most obvious—is what I call Body Wealth

This falls under that category of *Your Wealth* in the wealth circle. This, unfortunately, is a neglected area among many people, for one reason or the other. Many people are 'experts' in creating a healthy body, and new technologies, methods, and medications are coming up every day. The move now is toward staying healthy and a preventative approach to health. However, there are many existing approaches, which people do not try, due to the difficulty in achieving results. That is why people are looking for the easy way out of this highly important part of their wealth. There is no easy way out, and that is why so many people still struggle with their health. Suffice it to say that without your health, all wealth is useless to you.

In fig 1.1, you will see that it is called *Your Wealth*. This Is because it is the one wealth you get just by being born. I know some people don't start off with healthy bodies and minds, it is still the one way that is currently acceptable to exist on earth.

There are many resources that now work for the purpose of taking care of your body and your health. The one, which is somewhat controversial in South Africa, is *The Real Meal Revolution*, written by Jonno Proudfoot, Sally-Ann Creed, and Tim Noakes. This was a foreign concept to me, having spent my university years learning an opposing theory to nutrition than what was presented in the book. I was faced with the dilemma of following my heart or my head. I tried it, mainly due to my family risk factors: diabetes and hypertension, on both my mother's side and my father's side. Having used it for six months successfully to lose 12 kilograms of weight, while feeling energetic and strong, I had only one challenge: how to keep my desired weight as it is. I subsequently stopped using the program for this reason, and I went back to my original, overweight self. As I write now, I plan to create my own way of being healthy, which will allow me to maintain my weight where I desire it to be. This is neither a recommendation, nor an endorsement of any particular system, but, rather, sharing my own experience. It should therefore, not be taken as medical advice.

A mentor of mine has recommended *Body for Life*, a book and program by Bill Phillips. I am told this is a challenging program, but it works very well. It involves planning all your meals in advance for six days of the week, and having whatever you want on the seventh day. This is in addition to an extensive exercise regime. This has been praised by countless people, however, consistently being on this program was the challenge. This is not an exhaustive list of what is available out there, but an example of differing theories of health maintenance and weight loss, which work differently for different people.

There are two important points in this. Firstly, always be doing something that contributes to your health and wellbeing, no matter how small. Secondly, remember that it is not what works, but what duplicates that counts. What can you do—no matter how small—that will be consistent over the longest period of time?

Many people don't know what their ideal health is for and why they take care of their bodies. Some use it for their careers, particularly in sports, and stop as soon as they no longer are involved in sport. Others improve their health because it is the current trend or fad, others still do it because they realize the long-term effect of being healthy on their quality of life. You enjoy life more when your body and health are at their peak. If you don't agree, ask the sickly billionaire next door.

Soul Wealth

The next form of wealth we will speak of, which also falls under you, is Soul Wealth. This area covers your mind, emotions, and knowledge. This is the seat of human consciousness where we actually live. This is, by far, the area over which we have the most control, but exercise it the least. Building wealth in this area involves using your mind to its full potential. Your mind is a tool, in as much as your hands are. When you were born, you wondered what hands are and were surprised that you had them. Don't believe me? Look at how babies stare in awe at their own hands. It is with such awe that we view the mind when we are still young. Too many people—even in their old age—view it the same way. What should happen is that in the same way you spend time learning the things that your hands can do to the point of mastery, you should learn what your mind can do and master it.

The second part we have within the Soul is emotions, and these are the colors that make everyday living exciting. Imagine a world where everything happened as it does, but no emotions were ever attached to it. This world would be dreary, mechanical, and robotic, and the interactions between humans would be bleak, forced, and uninspiring. Emotions are as a result of chemical processes happening in your brain in the area called the Limbic System. You don't need to know about where it is and why it does what it does. It does, however, play a big role in your success in life and wealth creation. The most successful people and those who get ahead in life are not emotionless machines who only had money on their minds. They are people, like you and me, who have learned how to control their emotions in order to move forward in life, rather than allow the emotions to pull them back.

Does the JOB you do evoke emotions for you?

Why?

Does it evoke emotions that you desire?

Whatever the emotions, they are being embedded in your subconscious mind, and you are likely to attract more of it. If you want to change this, start now!

Knowledge Wealth

The final part that we will discuss is Knowledge wealth. The collection and use of knowledge are the core of human existence without which progress is not possible. The collective knowledge of humans in the current time is so vast that it is difficult to quantify. There is so much knowledge out there and so much to learn. Here is an analogy – whatever you know now about any topic can be said to be like the area your shadow covers compared to the entire earth. This means that whatever you have wondered about, someone out there knows the answer or is in the process of getting it. For our purposes, this is good news, especially relating to wealth and wealth creation. The people who have manifested

physical wealth in their lives started with knowledge wealth and, through action, converted that to physical wealth. You have heard many people say *knowledge is power*; however, if that were true, everyone who could acquire knowledge about wealth would be wealthy. The reality is that *knowledge is potential power*, and this potential lies with the person who gains such knowledge.

That is why different people get different outcomes, get different out comes using even when they're working with the same knowledge and skills. When I speak of knowledge, I am not speaking of intelligence as the world measures it. Far be it from me to convince you that the higher your IQ, or capacity to take up and use new concepts, the wealthier you will become. All you need is to spend enough time acquiring the right knowledge and concepts that will extract the wealthy person within you. Right for who? It must be right for you. Even amongst billionaires, they have different explanations, practices, and beliefs as to how they reached their current financial wealth. Learn from all of them, and practice all that is in common, and, then, take your path. You and I both are on a lifelong journey of learning how we can use what we have, along with what we learn, to create the lives we desire.

Spirit Wealth

The next form of wealth we will speak of is Spirit Wealth. There are three main people in this area. One who creates immense spiritual wealth, but struggles or negates any physical form of wealth. These people will usually also possess Soul Wealth, as the two are closely connected. However, they believe that accumulating any amount of material wealth will oppose the Spiritual Wealth they have acquired. The other group are opposed to anything spiritual, because of either past negative experiences with religion, or a personal choice to avoid it altogether. These people believe that there is nothing spiritual about wealth creation, and that they only need create material wealth to fulfil their dreams and desires.

The third finds a fluid balance between the two, which allows him to create wealth both spiritually and materially.

Which one is correct? I choose the third group, and I will assume you

will, too (since you are reading this book). Understand this: my position is not to convince you that religion is either right or wrong, but to convince you to decide whether your belief system will move you toward creating wealth or not. For certain people, spirituality is explored without a religious or faith-based pretext, and for others, this is fundamental – all are able to create spiritual and material wealth for as much as they can learn about who they are and how this fits in to the bigger picture of their wealth.

The internal world wealth and external world wealth need to be well-balanced, in order for true wealth to be created. This is the true wealth we desire. We will approach it in the direction that there is a building period during which you are laying the building blocks that will someday become your wealth skyscraper. There is no telling how long this period will last, as it differs for each individual. The question is, when you have discovered what your passion is and how you can become wealthy using this, will you burn out? I address this question very early, because it is one of the reasons some people never pursue wealth to begin with. The statement goes a little something like, "I would love to be wealthy someday, but I don't wanna kill myself". They are referring, ever-so-subtly, to the potential that everyone has for burnout from whatever they do.

Burnout

Let's start by defining burnout – Wikipedia (our other brain) says it's "a psychological term that refers to long-term exhaustion and diminished interest in work." It goes on to technicalities about how it comes about, and it mentions that you should seek assistance if you think you suffer from this condition. What is also mentioned is that burnout can result from many factors, not just workload. However, work seems to be the place easiest to notice decreased performance as a result of burnout. To answer our question, we must know what areas

people usually speak about it. The first is in their careers: just about any career can burn people out, due to the progressive nature of most careers and the demands they put on the people who do them willing or unwillingly. Also, the repetitive and tedious nature of most careers can discourage even the most enthused people, if they do it long enough or wrong enough.

Perhaps you feel it's not true and maybe it's a lot of hogwash. Well, here is an assignment for you. Find ten people you know personally to be wealthy or ten whom you learn about online. Find out which of those people created their wealth doing what they studied in college as their sole means of creating wealth. What you will find is that only a few people were able to create wealth solely using their college qualification, and that most added some other revenue streams to add to their careers. Still others did not even get to a career and created wealth with a brilliant idea that served others.

Look at Mark Zuckerberg, who created Facebook™, look at Bill Gates, look at Oprah Winfrey. The list is endless of people who didn't follow the regular path, but ended up successful.

You may say, the list is also endless of people who tried the same, but ended in disaster. That may well be true; these are the possibilities that can occur. Whatever you decide to create is what will become the reality. Choose today, and take the appropriate actions necessary.

In the situation that you have finally found your true passion and are creating the kind of wealth you desire using that passion, the reality is that you can still burn out. Passion is an inner world phenomenon existing in your mind. The more aligned it is to your outer world physical state, the less likely you will burnout.

Burnout is like a train moving at high speed as it approaches a tunnel. The driver, though experienced in all aspects of the train, its mechanics, and its dimensions, has never been to this tunnel and doesn't know its height. What will happen? What we know for sure is that the train has to stop. It can be voluntary or involuntary. The avoidance of burnout, therefore, is more about knowing yourself and your route. He may stop voluntarily and start changing the tunnel to suit his train, or find another means of getting past the tunnel. He may even decide that he wants to take another route the opposite way.

Let's take an example of an overweight young man who dreams of becoming a marathon runner. He may have invested a large amount of time improving his mind power to become emotionally and spiritually wealthy as an endurance runner. However, the elephant in the room, as it were, is that his body may not be able to keep up with his newfound mindset. In essence, it will cause him burnout to attempt running a marathon, which he may be mentally prepared for, but not physically prepared for. This, then, will require a steady improvement of the physical fitness, until it can endure what the mind is capable of.

This is fundamental to learn when creating success, too. Success—whether in the outer world or the inner world—needs to be matched with its counterpart. Material wealth needs to be matched with a wealthy mindset, so as to be effective. Conversely, creating mental wealth will surely bring about material wealth, but not automatically. There are still actions you must take to ensure that you create and sustain your wealth. This is critical knowledge and must be applied regularly to create mental wealth.

The way in which I theorize this is based on my experience as a medical student who got burned-out. Open up your mind to the possibility that you could be a totally different and happier person than you are now. If you think your current lifestyle brings you fulfillment, multiply that by a thousand, and you will get the potential you can have. Think about this often, and imagine this 1k person each day.

Life burnout

The most distressing form of burnout is life burnout. This is when life has become so dreary and boring that getting out of bed is mission impossible. We need be turning that to Mission I'm Possible. To avoid this kind of burnout, we must find our passion, however long it takes. We must be open to new possibilities and to our lives changing for the better. Then, we will make it happen and enjoy the process, too. We will do what I call *Burning the Burnout*. We will do this by finding new passions in different areas of life, so that we fulfill our life purpose and live significantly. More realistically, we will rediscover the passion in what we are currently doing. When we open our minds, we can walk into the same room twice and see completely different realities. We are those type of people. I say this to you not because I am trying to rile you up, but really to assist you in realizing that no matter where you are in life, there is more to be had, if you want it. Your life is not going to end in what it is now ,as long as you decide it isn't. All the answers are available. What questions are you asking?

Why do people gamble?

My personality type, which is Phlegmatic Sanguine, means that I love observing and analyzing people. One day, I went to the local casino alone and observed people who were gambling. I don't really gamble and don't have much use for it, but I wanted to understand why others do—and can even end up addicted to it. My conclusion, though not the only reason, is as follows: People who gamble have the inherent belief that they need lots of money very quickly. The second belief is that in order to do that, they need something which they can invest the lowest possible amount of time and money in order to get the biggest return. Thirdly, they believe that once they have the money they desire, they can stop gambling and get back to the 'mainstream' investment opportunities. Underlying this is a secondary belief system, namely that wealth comes with luck, which is an external force or a woman, Lady Luck, and if she is on your side, you will win. However, if bad luck, her evil twin, is on your side, you will lose. This belief creates a market for those who sell luck charms and other means of bringing lady luck closer, but with no guarantees. Others still believe that luck comes from an internal place that depends on how they feel, what they are wearing, and what the weather is like. All these beliefs put conditions that must be met before you can create gambling wealth, and your subconscious mind then extends these to all other things you do, even legitimate investments. This is the fundamental flaw with gambling and why it makes very few rich and even fewer sustainably wealthy.

Life is a gamble?

Why do casinos operate?

As I was looking at the gamblers and feeling sorry for them, I could not help feeling sorry for myself, because I used to live my life as a gamble. I looked with admiration at the casino as a business model. This is such a desirable business model that governments all over the world would want to strongly regulate and tax it. Let's look superficially at what they do and compare it to their customers:

- They are clear about why they are operating their business
- They put in years and years of research to understand how the games and machines they use will work.
- They spend large amounts of revenue learning about their customer, his habits, how he operates, and what would keep him coming back.
- They incentivize their customers to come and bring their families, which would otherwise be a reason for the customer to leave early.
- The casino then ensures that their customers win just enough to keep them hopeful, but lose enough to keep them gambling.
- They ensure that the barrier to entry is as low as possible so that their customers don't notice how much they are spending.
- They top it all off by operating for long periods of time in premises where it is difficult to notice that time is flying. Their customers will always increase their average spend per session and become repeat buyers.

If all other businesses had this model, the world would be a very different place. Now, this is not an attack on, nor endorsement of casinos, nor people who gamble with money, because all of us gamble with something in life. This is also not to say you can't gamble if you want to be wealthy. Gambling is neither good nor bad. The question is: does it move you forward or pull you back from your goals? If it pulls you back, you should stop it. If it moves you forward, then, by all means, go ahead. The above analysis may change as I study more into this, but there are, however, two important messages. Firstly, the loss of money in gambling is not the worst thing that can happen to you; losing money is relative to how much you have. It is the destruction of important relationships as a result of the loss of money or assets. It is also the subconscious belief that wealth comes from luck. This belief may affect your ability to create and maintain wealth in other areas of life, outside of material wealth. Secondly, wealth is attracted

to those who are prepared for it in the inner world. Those who believe that it is abundant and not scarce.

The Abundancy and Scarcity of Wealth

There is a paradox in wealth creation, namely that if you think there is an abundance of wealth in the world, you are correct, and if you think there is a scarcity of wealth, you are correct, too. The only thing is that you cannot entertain both views. Which will you be in your life? The gambler or casino? The reality is that you find what you seek. If you seek a small portion of an abundant financial wealth, you will find more than you expected. If, however, you desire a large portion of scarce financial resources, you are likely to get even less than you expected. You will always find what you seek, and it will remain true, even if you live in a place where others think wealth is abundant, until the day you decide that it is abundant. Ironically, if you come from a scarcity mentality, those with an abundant mentality only confirm your scarcity thoughts until you change your own perspective.

You create your reality with the thoughts you entertain daily. Perhaps you have a business, and you are considering partnering with a bigger business. You know that you have to give up shares or equity for the investment that this partner will make. A scarcity mentality wants to own 100 percent, because this new partner will 'use you to get rich'—essentially, there is a small pie, and you must keep all of it for as long as possible. An abundant mentality believes that the pie will grow and be huge and that giving away 50 percent of a huge pie is better than keeping 100 percent of no pie. This does not mean you don't do your due diligence, it just means you open your mentality to the abundance that exists all around you. If you desire abundance, you must think abundant thoughts and act in an abundant way.

Wealth and abundance, therefore, cannot be separated. John Kehoe says that abundance is the law of the universe, and this law applies to your thoughts, your words, and your actions. It applies

to your inner and outer worlds. It punishes those who choose to ignore it by giving them an abundance of whatever they think about most of the time. It rewards those who pay attention to it by giving them an abundance of whatever they think about most of the time.

If you read the last two sentences twice and thought it was a typo, it wasn't. In the law of abundance, the punishment and the reward are the same. However, you choose which it is that you will get. If you choose to pay attention to this law and think the thoughts, speak the words, and walk the walk of abundance, you will be richly rewarded with whatever you desired. You will hold the power to create. If, however, you entertain thoughts of scarcity, speak mediocrity, and walk in conformity, you will receive an abundance of those things. You get what you deserve.

Deserving Wealth

As I mentioned before, James McNiel says de-serving comes as a result of serving. Whatever you 'serve' most at, you 'de- serve'. If you say you deserve respect, it must be because you serve respect in everything you do. The ability to spell the word doesn't make you deserve it, regardless of what respect means to you. Zig Ziglar speaks of the same thing when he says, "You can get anything you want in life, as long as you help enough other people get what they want."

This can be applied to wealth creation in a big way. We can learn how people who are wealthy now came to be so, who they helped in life. Most will tell you that they desired, decided, became deliberate, did, and duplicated. This created the wealth that they have now. Most people end at the desire, but no matter how great it is, it cannot create wealth. We must then model wealth using the Buffalo Question.

The Buffalo Question

There is a saying in isiZulu that says, "Inyathi ibuzwa kwaba phambili," meaning that you ask those who are ahead in your path if there are dangers to foresee, like a buffalo, which may attack you. I will take this further to say that because you can ask them, it is likely that they have overcome the buffalo and come out alive. If had they not, you would not be able to ask them. They probably found great insight into how to avoid the buffalo, insights which could ensure that if you were to meet two buffalo, you would be able to subdue them both, and maybe even sell them for a tidy sum. Furthermore, if the people ahead could overcome said buffalo, then, being human like them, you will be able to be just as good at overcoming—or even better. By the time you meet the buffalo, you will not be alone. Instead, you will have the insights and methods of all those who contributed to the Buffalo Answer, which you now possess. Finally, if you have received the Buffalo Answer, you have the responsibility to help others who have the Buffalo Question.

Wisdom is learning from your mistakes, genius is learning from the mistakes of others. Be a genius in everything you do. Model excellence in everything you do. This means that you should find mentors who are doing what you want to do. Model what they do exactly at first, then, once you have mastered it, modify or flavor it to your requirements. Many people modify what they have not mastered. Think of a medical student learning from a surgery professor how to remove the appendix. He should learn to master the tried-and-tested technique taught to him and, then, he can come up with a new—and possibly better—way to do it.

Kaizen

Once you have found a person to ask the Buffalo Question – namely, a mentor—and have also modelled and mastered what they do, you are now ready to apply the Japanese principle of Kaizen.

This is the principle that in whatever you do, you should improve in small increments over a long period of time and eventually, without effort, you will find yourself at higher and higher levels of mastery. This is in contrast to haphazard improvements and regressions that may prove difficult for wealth creation. Kaizen is eating the elephant piece by piece, rather than eating it all on your birthday. This principle is taught in an excellent way in the book *The Slight Edge,* by Jeff Olsen.

All true wealth is represented by Kaizen. One dollar at a time until you have a million of them. Each day, you should add an increment of the wealth in all aspects of your life. How do you know what an increment is? What is it measured against? Your values. They will determine what your goals are. Your actions, therefore, will represent what results you desire. The frequency and massiveness of the actions will be determined by what you desire the results to be.

You Always Win

I am a believer that you always win in everything you do. You started your life as a winner, why should your life end any differently? I am referring to your conception, where you competed with more than 250 million other sperm for the ultimate prize – your mother's ovum. Without your determination, you couldn't be reading this today. Take a moment to think about this and acknowledge yourself for this. It is, therefore, my opinion that you are predisposed to winning and that your victorious end will come, regardless of any obstacles that may come your way. The only person who is a loser is the one who doesn't see the victories that are right in front of them. These people think their victory is coming someday, will be brought by someone, and will only last for some time. This is flawed thinking, and, as such, one who thinks like that is bound to create that reality for themselves.

"So, 'Mr. Know-It-All'," I hear you say under your breath, "How, exactly, should I think, because my life doesn't show signs of victory? In fact, quite the opposite." Well, dear friend, my job is not to tell you how to think, but to remind you that if the thoughts create the reality and, then, the reality reinforces the thoughts. It stands to reason, therefore, that if you change your thoughts to victorious ones, after a time, the reality will follow suit, and by so doing, create a victory cycle with thoughts of victory producing a victorious reality, and, in turn, creating more thoughts of victory.

So, you ask, "Does that mean I can magically think good and positive thoughts and my life will change forever and I will live happily ever after?" It will never happen that you will not experience challenges or even problems. Indeed, your winning mentality started in the race you won against millions of others. Once born, your competition is against yourself or yourselves.

You continue asking questions and say, "Who are these other selves?" Well, how I look at it is that the thoughts you think create new dimensions, in which you have the potential to follow certain thoughts leading to different results in each dimension or universe. This is because even while you think five thoughts about what you will do in the next five minutes, only one of those thoughts will actually be actioned by you. Depending on which thought you choose, the resulting paths that open are different and will produce different outcomes. The question you should ask yourself is which of those thoughts and subsequent actions will result in your success and your wealth. So, in effect, you have a competition going on within and whoever wins your thoughts, words, and actions ultimately wins. So, who will it be? The small-minded, fearful, scared you? Or will it be the victorious warrior champion you were born to be?

Stay winning

Here are some easy steps to become and stay a winner:

Step 1 - Make winning easy by realizing that all the small wins in your life are what make you a true winner. I would prefer to have one small win daily for a year than to have one big win every month for a year. The journey needs to be a victory-filled one for the destination to feel like a worthwhile one. This doesn't mean the journey needs to be easy. It does need to be rewarding, though.

Step 2 – Remember that even when other people win, you also win. If someone like Elon Musk can create some of the biggest and most innovative businesses in the world, then even you can. He is human as you are, has the same life challenges you do, and can still manage to achieve greatness. Therefore, always take other people's wins as your own, starting with people who you have the most in common with. If they won, celebrate, because it shows that you, too, if you develop your potential to the fullest, will win. Once you create the circumstances necessary to win, it's only a matter of time.

Step 3 – Celebrate all wins. This is a principle that Blair Singer teaches as part of Little Voice Mastery. Your brain works with positive reinforcement, so the more you celebrate, the more your brain wants to celebrate. The more you find small things to celebrate about, the more you create opportunities for bigger celebrations. It links in with gratitude, which we mentioned earlier. The more grateful you are for the little things, the more likely the universe will give you bigger things to be grateful about. This is an irrefutable principle, which you use in your own life every day, even if you didn't notice it before.

These three steps will keep you on the winning streak always. What happens when something doesn't go your way? Is that a win, too? Well, it all depends how you react to it. If there is a lesson to be learned, then, you win, because in the future, that same lesson may be worth a lot more to you when you avoid the same mistake on a bigger scale or when you teach others how to avoid it.

Preparations for wealth

Like everything worth doing, there are preparations which are needed for wealth that everyone needs before creating it. Almost all wealthy people make these preparations whether consciously or unconsciously. These preparations are what make wealth a reality. Dr. John Demartini speaks of people who have dreams, desires, and goals but are unwilling to pay the necessary price. It is only when you determine what the price is, and you make up your mind to pay that price that you have started making those dreams, desires, and goals achievable. Consider the below formula:

Dreams + Desires = **Fantasies**

Fantasy + Action = **Reality**

Inner wealth preparation

In his book *The Millionaire Within*, Andrew Barsa eludes to the four areas of the self where wealth is created, namely the spiritual, the soul, the emotional, and the physical. Now, all these have a big role to play in your wealth; however, three are in the inner world. Most people focus on the physical world and totally ignore the other more important three. T. Harv Eker uses an analogy of your inner world being like the container for your wealth. The bigger the container, the more wealth it can contain and, more importantly, keep. The smaller the container, the more inevitable the reality of all the wealth flowing out of the container. This is true in everyday life, so why wouldn't it be true for wealth? He speaks further to say that the Universe doesn't accommodate a vacuum, so if you have a big wealth container and you don't yet have the wealth, then it's just a matter of time before the wealth is attracted to the container.

Therefore, focusing on increasing the capacity of your container is the best inner world preparation you can do before you can create your wealth. Reading a book such as *Mind Power,* by John Kehoe, will help you increase the capacity of your container, and, eventually, you will realize that the inner world is where true wealth is stored up. There are questions you need to ask yourself in this preparation. I have listed them in order of the importance I give to them:

Why do you want to create wealth?

The clearer you are about this question, the more likely you are to achieve the goals, even against strong criticism and opposition. The people you look up to who created wealth of any kind knew precisely why they wanted to create wealth and why nothing and, indeed, no one would stop them. I will say this: no one is trying to stop you becoming wealthy. No one except yourself—in particular, your mind. If you overcome your own opposition to your wealth, you can overcome anything and anyone. Focus on reasons that benefit you, those around you, and those in your future.

Outer wealth preparation

Outer wealth preparation involves learning the skills and knowledge required to make wealth in the current time period. In each time period, the vehicles used to create wealth change and increase, however, the preparation still remains the same. You can imagine that businesses and real estate are the oldest form of wealth creation vehicles, and paper assets, like stocks, unit trusts, and mutual funds are a more modern form of wealth creation. Historically, however, the principle remains the same that everything that can create wealth can create bankruptcy, and vice versa. The deciding factor between people who create one, rather than the other, is the preparation in the inner world and the outer world.

Inner world preparation

The inner world preparations include learning from people who have achieved what you want to achieve and modelling them and finding personal mentors who will guide you through the process and help you with questions that you may have. These are questions of being, who you must become to be the wealthy you. Remember, all mentors and teachers can do is to guide you – there is still the physical and mental action that you must take that makes the result belong to you. Many people make the mistake of thinking mentors are people who do things for you – those are employees – mentors are advisors. You still need to make a decision based on the best information available to you at the time. Sometimes, it works, sometimes, it doesn't. What lesson did you learn? How did you win?

The more preparation you put into the inner world, the more you magnify the results you can create in the outer world. This leads to the final wealth, which I consider complete wealth.

Complete Wealth

This is the synergy of the inner and outer world wealth. Think of it as a cycle, rather than a linear continuum – see fig 8.1

Desired wealth should always precede achieved or actual wealth.

This wealth is not limited to the financial wealth, but to any form of wealth, as in Fig. 8.1 above. The requirement is that the desire be clarified in the thoughts and emotion centers. This can be achieved using mind power and meditation techniques. Brian Tracy refers to this as the mental equivalent for the actual wealth. Without a mental or inner world equivalent, your wealth will not be created—or if it is, by chance, it will not sustain itself. There is usually a deliberate and consistent action that goes into the journey from desired or inner wealth to the achieved or outer wealth. After the outer wealth is achieved, however, there is an increase in desire for more of the same wealth or a different kind of wealth that you consider more valuable than the first. This is why it seems that people will seek something so passionately when they don't have it, but soon come to take it for granted once they have it. Jim Carey says this of financial wealth, "I wish everyone would become millionaires, so that they would realize that it's not the answer." The trick is to enjoy both journeys, especially the one from the inner world to the outer world. This is a special kind of wealth, which stands on its own and can be learned. I call it Journey Wealth.

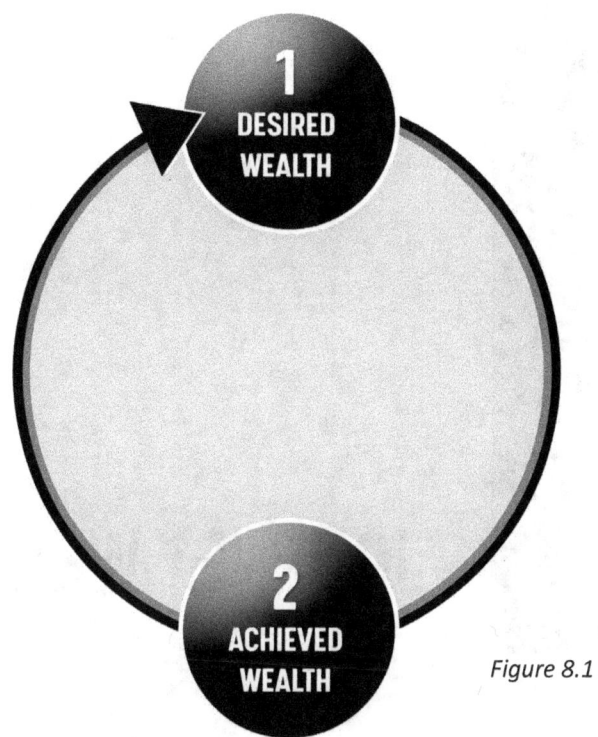

Figure 8.1

Up Next

In the last chapter, we will wrap up the content of the book, and look at Journey Wealth. This is a neglected form of wealth, but, due to its abundant nature, it is one you will need to focus on, if you are to achieve the Stop Working, Get Wealthy dream.

CHAPTER 9
JOURNEY WEALTH

This is probably the most misunderstood form of wealth. So misunderstood that most people would shun it off as suffering, rather than wealth. Think of this wealth as the canvas on which a masterpiece is drawn, the long flight to the paradise destination that you dreamed of for life, or even the waiting period for your dream house. All these fill every aspect of our lives and some of them are mundane, while others are difficult—even excruciating, but the results of all of them move you ever-closer to your desired goal. It is the desired goal that can change. The existence of the journey can never be omitted, so have fun during this phase of the dream, too – once you do, you can never consider yourself disadvantaged.

One of the things we do that lead to the desired wealth is personal development. This is the process you go through in order become the kind of person who does the kind of things needed to get what they want. An example of this is a person who wants to be a millionaire. Traditional teaching and society say this person needs to have a million dollars, then he can do what millionaires do, and, then, he will be a millionaire. It sounds plausible and logical to the untrained mind; however, it works for less than one percent of people.

Be to Do to Have

Personal development teaches that you need to be a millionaire in your thoughts and beliefs and do the things that millionaires do, and, then, you will have a million dollars. "Ridiculous!" you say? "If it were that simple, everyone would be a millionaire." Well, maybe it is, and I say this tongue in cheek. Perhaps we have complicated the process. Here is my theory about how two people in a relationship can create the best relationship for themselves. Individually, they need to be the perfect partners they desire in the other person i.e. honest, loving, selfless, and reliable. They, in fact, need to believe that this relationship is the best and begin to act as though it is by doing the things they would do in the best relationship. Then, as though by magic, they will have the best relationship. Having always comes after being and doing. In traditional terms, people believe that when they have the best partner, they will be the best partners for them, and they will do what best partners do. This is flawed thinking, and I have practiced it many times, myself. The sooner we overcome such a mindset, the quicker we get to the wealth we desire and escalate to even greater wealth to create.

Think about this, and practice it as a law in everything you do. When you do this over a period of time, you realize that there is no other way of doing anything. This is a bold statement to make; however, if you have been doing things another way, and it hasn't been working, try this way.

Journey to Being

In life, you may have a lot to loose, but nothing to lose. First, I am deliberately using the word loose, instead of lose, because I have seen it being done in my local area. It's an interesting word to use, not because it's a spelling error, but because it reminds one of a biblical application of the word. The Bible speaks about things that are loosed on earth shall be loosed in heaven. This speaks of the power of the spoken word and is application to preparing the inner world to change things in the outer world. I am not giving a lesson in biblical interpretation; however, instead of losing anything in life, always think of loosing it. In other words, you have not lost, but have an opportunity to loose the situation, which seems like a loss.

I believe that there are no losses in life. I believe there are no failures. Only opportunities to get feedback and try again as a better you. We have no idea how much what we call 'failures' shape who we become. Show me the power of a person who has never lost and never failed, and I will show you Nelson Mandela, Mahatma Gandhi, and Dr. Martin Luther King Jr. These are examples of people considered to have lost and failed initially, but who won the legacy of staying in the hearts, minds, and lips of humans for generations to come. The one thing they all had in common which ensured they never lost, but loosed, was their fierce focus on a greater good—sometimes, a good that they would never get to see or feel.

Your focus is the one thing people can never take away from you. People may see different things happen in your life, but only you know what parts of the masterpiece these create. You cannot compete with anyone but yourself. Your focus is your compass. Some may call this your vision and others your goal. It is the all-encompassing thing you plan to achieve, no matter what comes your way. Firstly, if you don't already have one, make it your first goal to find it. How? Go to the resources section.

Many people may say they find it difficult to focus on one thing. They find that they may start something, but not finish it. This a highly frowned upon, because it may mean you are unreliable, uninterested, or lacking drive. I put it down to another reason: it is not something that you want to do. This doesn't mean that you shouldn't do it. There may be many rational reasons why you should, reasons that make a lot of sense. However, the sooner you find another, more enjoyable, way of doing what you need to do in the way that you want to, the more enjoyable the journey will be.

Let's take an example of money in as far as it allows you to make a living. It is inescapable that in the world today, you need money to carry on a reasonable existence – though in the context of this book, this is never your goal. We can, therefore, assume that you need to make money. This can be done by taking up a difficult job that supplies enough for said existence at the cost of requiring all of your time. You would not be blamed for wanting to leave that job to look for something better. On the other hand, if you had found something that you wanted to do that paid the same amount, you would be unlikely to look for something better. Instead, you would look for ways to maximize and leverage what you currently do.

A saying goes, "There are no lazy people, only people who have not discovered their passion in life!"

We have covered everything regarding getting wealthy. Now, to finalize the book with the origin of the idea...

Stop Working

Remember the train approaching the tunnel? If you found the title of this book interesting, it is because you are approaching one in your life. You are at a fork in the road. It's time to stop! Don't quit your JOB just yet, but stop.

If you think you are in the wrong JOB, you are right. One of two things

must happen. A better version of you needs to show up at work ,or you need to show up at a better job. The first prize is a better version of you showing up at a better job. Sometimes, all this takes place in the place where you are right now.

A job here can be traditional employment, self-employment, or even a fully-fledged business.

A Better You

You become a better you when you know yourself better. When you understand that you are a powerful creator in your own life. That you already possess the tools to create all the things that you want in life. You may have been using them without knowing you are in control.

First, be you.

There is no one as unique as you. No one who can do what you were meant to do, in the scale, area, and for the duration that you were meant to. It was only meant for you. How lovely would it be if, for the first time, you could meet your true self? Unburdened by what others will say or think, to finally walk the path of discovering who you are. And once you discover you, never looking back. Being is the ultimate part of your existence. Without it, you are not.

Next, do you.

No-one will ever truly understand what you need to do in the world, except you. Doing should always flow from being. Because only you can be you, only you can do you. Having said that, the skills required to do what you need to are already known by others in the world (most of the time). The difference is that they are not allocated the same scale, area, and duration that you are.

Finally, have you.

If you put effort into the two parts above, then having is a result. A prize, as it were. You will have what you truly desire. Why? Because the real you wants the best things for you. As a result, you will do what's best for you, so that what you will end up with is what you desired.

Take heed: you need to find the real you. Use tools that help you discover your personality, your values, your temperament, and your wealth personality. Keep doing these, because you change ever-so-slightly over time.

A Better JOB

To me, a JOB is a means to an end.

What function does the JOB fulfil? It needs to allow you to be better at being you. It should reward you for serving the universe with your gift. It should recognize your uniqueness and reinforce it. Next, it should remunerate you appropriately. Remunerate? Yes, sometimes more money isn't the answer, particularly if the nature of your JOB doesn't allow for you to be you. Then, giving you more time to yourself, so you can be you, would be the ultimate remuneration. Research has shown that some people would prefer more time off than a salary increase. I say it's because money is also a means to an end.

We want it to do something with it.

A JOB should always speak to the three parts of you and in addition to that, be able to grow you. How? By allowing you to discover more parts about yourself than you knew existed. Some of the best work environments in the works look more like spaces you would normally find humans in. Not cube-shaped, compartmentalized cells.

A better JOB should also be able to incorporate more the thing that occupies your mind the most. For most people, it's family. Many JOBs could not care less about your family, while others make it an integral part. Which do you think would help you be a better you? If you are a better you at work, what will the company gain more of?

Most JOBs are functions of businesses. They can, therefore, be seen as individual businesses functioning in concert. Even a person who has never run a business knows that it is done differently from being an employee in a business. You have to be the business, do the things that you need to do on the business to finally have a real business. You need to be self- driven, focused, and inspired from within from a place of true purpose for you to run a successful business.

What if everyone thought of their JOB as their business. What if your employer gave you a business plan for your function, rather than a JOB description? What if your salary was related to your performance in your JOB and how this all fit into the bigger picture? You may say, "But this is already happening." It is, but even the bigger companies cannot show the employee the bigger picture and the ultimate impact his or her JOB has on the world. This would mean businesses would need to be more ethical, thoughtful, and meaningful to the world for people to feel a sense of true purpose in their JOBs.

If your JOB is your business, how much should you love your business? Since your JOB is your business, like most small Businesses, the owner is the only employee. What is the ideal employee to work in your business? Since you are the boss of your one (wo)man business, is it okay that your employee is gossiping about you? Are you the ideal employee? Would you like to have an employee in your business who hates the JOB they have, but stays in anyway, so they can pay the bills?

Ask these questions, and you will realize that you have always had the answer. Before you start blaming your JOB and plan your greener pastures exit, remember that you take yourself everywhere. Are you the best employee? Would you employ you? We normally have a bias towards our own abilities and strengths, so don't just take your own answer. Ask your colleagues, close friends, and family. Their answers will give you a good idea.

This reminds me of the man who hated fish. One day, a man came home from work. He was walking in through the gate, and suddenly, a pungent fish smell overcame him. He could not stand the smell, so he walked faster toward the front door. The smell was getting stronger. He thought the smell must be coming from inside the house. He entered and saw his wife, who was watching television.

"Can you smell that?" he asked his wife.

"No, honey, are you hungry?" she asked.

"Famished!" he replied. "Did you make fish?!" She looked at him, puzzled.

"I know how much you hate it, so no. Why do you ask?"

He was looking around frantically and sniffing everything. "Everything smells like FISH! I hate it, and I'm leaving."

His wife folded her arms, looked at him, and sarcastically said, "You might want to remove the fish stuck to your jacket, first. Otherwise, everything, including the pub, will smell like fish."

*There are no lazy people,
only people who have not become one
with their true purpose*

www.getwealthybook.com

ABOUT THE AUTHOR

They say an apple a day keeps the doctor away...not me!

I am a medical doctor, speaker, author, firewalking instructor, consultant and digital entrepreneur.

I have taken the lessons learnt from the obstacles in my own journey to help others in their businesses and their lives.

I wrote the book 3 years ago and decided to spend this time applying it to my own life before ever selling the first copy.

Wouldn't you rather read a book who's author has applied his own advice and produced results?

I am a strong believer in taking action and teaching, while you learn, I believe that change leaders are born everyday. Among my many passions I love helping people get better at being themselves because through this, the world will have people inspired to change for the better.

Is it time for a change?

www.ingramcontent.com/pod-product-compliance
Lightning Source LLC
LaVergne TN
LVHW011720060526
838200LV00051B/2965